ASCENT FROM DARKNESS

Memoirs of a young airline pilot's struggles with, and ultimate triumph over, a debilitating illness of the mind

by

Captain Al Kent

Bloomington, IN   authorHOUSE®   Milton Keynes, UK

AuthorHouse™   AuthorHouse™ UK Ltd.
1663 Liberty Drive, Suite 200   500 Avebury Boulevard
Bloomington, IN 47403   Central Milton Keynes, MK9 2BE
www.authorhouse.com   www.authorhouse.co.uk
Phone: 1-800-839-8640   Phone: 08001974150

ISBN: 978-1-4259-7577-7 (sc)
First published by AuthorHouse 3/29/2007

Library of Congress Control Number: 2006910491

Printed in the United States of America
Bloomington, Indiana

This book is printed on acid-free paper.

capt_al@ascentfromdarkness.net

CONTENTS

CHAPTER ONE
INTRODUCTION

Families all over the United States have experienced personal challenges when their loved ones become afflicted with a debilitating mental illness. Facing the daily struggles involved with the diagnosis and treatment for these afflictions of the mind can be very overwhelming, physically exhausting and even mentally draining at times. America's increasing number of mental health patients coupled with the staggering estimates of unreported depression has caused many experts in the mental health field to classify these problems as an epidemic in our society. It is estimated that the numbers of individuals who suffer from some form of depression and have not actively sought treatment number in the millions. In addition to the intangible tolls regarding human factors, depression alone has been said to create several billion dollars in lost productivity to our nation's economy each year.

During recent years, several individuals have made valiant efforts toward achieving a better understanding of the tremendous impact that mental health issues have upon our way of life. One of these mental health pioneers was former Surgeon General David Satcher, M.D., Ph. D. Dr. Satcher's passionate concern for our nation's mental wellness was never more evident when in 1999 he published a report titled "Call to Action to Prevent Suicide." The former Surgeon General's attention to the issues surrounding illnesses of the mind has allowed remarkable strides in recognizing the real epidemic that faces this country. In his 1999 suicide prevention report, Dr. Satcher wrote:

> *"Tragic and devastating mental disorders affect nearly one in five Americans in any given year, yet continue too frequently to be spoken of in whispers and shame."* [1]

His focus on mental health issues helped open the eyes of many individuals to the seriousness of the situation. However, remaining negative attitudes, common misunderstandings and discriminatory practices have created tremendous barriers to those seeking help for medical deficiencies of the brain, unarguably the most important organ in the complex human body.

Far too many men, women and children in the United States and around the world are forced to face their battles against mental illness while confronted with insurmountable odds and ridiculous barriers placed in their way by the inadequacies of an uncaring system. Fighting an illness of the mind is difficult enough without exasperating the situation by making these often fragile patients cope with marginal health providers, squabble with discriminatory insurance carriers and having their peers and co-workers often view them as being of "a lesser God." At a time when all energy should be spent on fighting the demon within, many individuals suffering a mental illness are tossed to the wind as being of weak character or are cast out labeled as societal failures. The tremendous financial burden of getting quality treatment adds to the anxiety and fear compounding the issues, enabling the illness to gain a tighter choke hold. The number of Americans, especially youth, attempting suicide is alarming.

---

[1]   "Our Mental Health Awards," <u>Psychology Today</u>. May/June 2000, pg. 46

Our elected officials must wake up to the realization of this giant disease that has gripped our society and aggressively treat this societal cancer that robs so much life and energy from all institutions. We, the people, must hold our leaders accountable to the task of making monumental improvements in order to stem this rising tide that leads so many children of God to succumb to such tragic and undesirable consequences. A kinder, gentler America can be achieved by breaking down the walls that have created massive voids between members of our society having serious medical conditions and the unfortunate individuals afflicted with devastating mental illnesses.

Ascent from Darkness is a factual representation of my life thus far and a collection of writings on which I have worked over time in anticipation of compiling a project that would serve as an accurate account of my life. Most of the names in this memoir have been changed to protect the identity of friends, family members and even myself in an attempt to avoid further discrimination and ostracizing that occurs from the horrible stigmas and misjudgments that unfortunately still surround illnesses of the mind. This book is a personal testament to the amazing power that lies within each of us allowing triumph over seemingly insurmountable odds. This autobiographical memoir is a first hand account of how a modest young man weathered a devastating bout of major depression and conquered the ensuing roller coaster ride from an inherited medical illness known as "bipolar disorder."

Bipolar disorder, traditionally referred to as "manic depression," is a medical condition that afflicts several million Americans. Significant evidence exists pointing to the fact that bipolar disorder is a hereditary illness passed from generation to generation and has been found to be most dominant on the male gene. The illness is usually characterized by mood swings having high amplitude, often cycling from deep depression (lows) to elated or euphoric states (highs). With varying severity levels, often the illness hides in wait until a significant life event creates high stress levels, manifesting itself only after such a triggering circumstance. Bipolar disorder is a highly treatable illness once properly diagnosed. Advances in medications used to treat manic depression have improved the success of bipolar patients to respond quicker and with more dramatic results. After the right medication is identified, most bipolar individuals are able to lead normal, productive and fulfilling lives.

Left untreated, many bipolar individuals turn to drinking and illegal drugs in an attempt to numb the pain of depression and sedate the manic tendencies. Often this dangerous mix of alcohol and non-prescribed narcotics has very negative social and even tragic long-term consequences. Many manic depressive individuals who are unable to receive proper treatment, refuse to maintain a regular medicine regimen, or are unaware of valuable support networks providing on-going therapy end up in very dire circumstances. Some untreated bipolar patients often resort to violence and criminal activity while many others end up tragically taking their own lives.

The primary purpose of this autobiography is to serve as an inspiration to the many individuals who find themselves plagued by the darkness often accompanying these gripping illnesses of the mind. My personal recollections and stimulating experiences should illustrate the fact that even when all seems lost, the power to rise above the worst afflictions is instilled within one's own being. Ominous storm clouds of depression often roll in and literally destroy all vibrancy life has to offer; however, let the accounts of my life serve as a constant reminder that the dark clouds will eventually part, exposing you to the warmth and glow of an awakening sunshine. If you are currently experiencing the depths of depression, I pray that the radiant light which now brightens my life will eventually shine down upon you and lift you from the depths of your personal trials.

Triumphing over the darkness of depression did not occur without the wonderful support of many individuals in my life. Loving family, devoted friends, remarkable pastors, exceptional physicians, caring counselors and the wonders of modern medicine all played an important part in helping me return from the engulfing darkness that once imprisoned my entire being. Most importantly, the devout faith that was developed through my trials and tribulations paved the path that brought me back to fullness once again. Please know, without a doubt, that you are never alone in your fight to rise out of the shadows that may be currently darkening your everyday life. By reaching out and grabbing the lifelines your loved ones have extended and by hanging prayerfully onto your faith, you too can persevere and rise above the storms that may be clouding your life with unbearable darkness.

There are many key players in this account of my life, but none are more important than my wonderful parents. I am extremely blessed to have such a remarkable mother and father who set the bar so high in being not only great parents, but also in exceeding all expectations for being charitable, caring and model human beings. They continue to be extremely supportive and inspirational and they will be loved eternally. Attempting to be as great a parent as my mom and dad have been to me is a nearly impossible task, but I try to be the best father I can be to my two boys. Spending as much time as possible with them is a priority in my life, and I am willing to sacrifice some of my own needs and desires to be the greatest possible dad.

What follows is my story of how a sleeping giant awoke, took control of my life and turned my world upside down. Through faith in God, tremendous support from my family and deep-down perseverance, I triumphed over an illness that for so many has lead to often tragic circumstances. I have had many friends and relatives who were not as fortunate in their personal struggles, having lost the battle to the darkness. Their memories are cherished and their spirits are undoubtedly responsible for leading me to write about my experiences. May God bless their souls and comfort their loved ones.

Ascent from Darkness is dedicated to the loving memory of my big brother Jeffrey Kent whose unsuccessful battle with a paralyzing case of manic depression cut short his life in 1981 at the age of twenty-one.

Chapter Two
The Glory Years

In the early winter of 1965, I arrived into this world to two loving parents living in a small rural community in southeastern Pennsylvania. The third of what would eventually be four boys, I was quite an energetic and adventurous child. My upbringing was fairly ordinary and my family lived very modestly as my father was a carpenter and my mother a homemaker and part-time restaurant waitress. Thankfully, I was a healthy young boy and have very fond memories of my early childhood. With two bigger brothers to keep me in line, a younger brother to push around a little, and two busy yet extremely compassionate parents, my life was fairly typical of the average American child. The more I think about it, above average would better describe my upbringing. Having participated in sports at a very early age, my parents deserve commendation for running me to all the practices and games while keeping a houseful of four boys under control. Life was good! I was an educated, happy, and active young boy; however, my usually well-adjusted demeanor would sometimes be replaced with urges for a sense of thrill and excitement.

When I was approximately nine years old, I began to idolize the once famous daredevil and motorcycle jumper Evel Knievel. Seeing him do his jumps on television was very exciting, and I tried to imitate his thrilling success as a stuntman at an early age. While most kids were riding their bikes around the neighborhood as a means of transportation and to have fun, my bicycle became a magnificent flying machine used to propel myself over almost anything and everything that I could build a ramp in front of. During a special fourth grade school event billed as the "Circus of the Stars," I donned a motorcycle helmet and did a jump in the school gym/cafeteria with the entire elementary student body, teachers and administrators watching. What a thrill! Can you imagine what would happen if a fourth grader wished to attempt such a stunt today? An act of Congress would probably not even allow such an event to take place on school grounds in present times. How our litigious world has changed, but that is a subject for another place and another time. I share this fascination with Mr. Knievel to illustrate a very lasting memory that brought my jumping days to an end.

A few years later after having jumped almost everything I could imagine, including my brother's '66 Chevelle Super Sport, I excitedly began to plan my biggest jump ever. I was to race down our long driveway, proceed through the garage and hit the ramp I had constructed at the back door that would launch me out into the backyard some eight to ten feet into the air. It was a magnificent plan modeled after Knievel's 1968 jump at Caesar's Palace in Las Vegas, Nevada. Unfortunately, one very important fact and critical calculation was missed in my preparation. I failed to realize that the opening in the rear of the garage where I was planning to catapult out had a door frame which was slightly narrower than my oversized bicycle handle bars. As I sped down the drive into the garage, my adrenaline was rushing as the thrill of this spectacular jump approached. When I hit the ramp pedaling at full speed, the thrill reached its climax as my handle bars slammed into the door jam and the bike instantaneously came to a stop. There is a saying in physics that "a body in motion will remain in motion..." Like a human cannonball, I was flung forward over the handle bars and through the back door, landing quite some distance down the hill in our backyard. Luckily, I was not severely injured, just some bumps and bruises. On that day the previous fascination with Mr. Knievel's exciting daredevil stunts came to an abrupt end, and my bicycle jumping addiction was henceforth permanently cured.

Two additional childhood memories are shared here for the benefit of my mother, who was raised a "plain sect" Mennonite and is still a vivacious character. These are a few of her favorites that she still reminds me about to this day: First of all, as early as I can remember, I was always keenly interested in the activities of my big brothers. When I was in middle school, one morning while getting ready to go to school, I was very curious as to the noise and commotion going on out in our driveway. Finishing my shower, I decided to peek out the bathroom window to see what my brothers were up to. As I climbed up on the towel rack, I briefly got a glimpse of them warming up their motorcycles as they were preparing to leave for high school. Briefly is the key word.

While witnessing the roar of the cycles' engines, the towel rack suddenly gave way and I plummeted to the floor of the bathroom, hitting the back of my head into an unknown sharp object. As the weight of my body hit the floor, my mother was alerted to the problem, hearing a very large thump from above as she was downstairs in the kitchen. When she arrived at the top of the steps and peered into the bathroom, I was laying in a fairly significant pool of blood, whimpering a lowly moan. Needless to say, after going to the doctor's office for several stitches to the back of my head and missing school for the day, the fact that towel racks were not designed to hold the weight of a young boy was painfully beat into my head. From that day on, I never again attempted to stand on another towel rack.

The second youthful adventure I would like to share begins when I was approximately fourteen years old. My parents had gone out for the evening leaving my younger brother and me home alone. After getting up the nerve to actually attempt a seriously deceptive deed, we headed for the garage, raised the garage door and proceeded to get into our family's 1970 Chevrolet™ station wagon. As I backed out the driveway, we were planning to go for a little "joy ride" in the green Chevy wagon. Accelerating down the road away from our home was both exciting and breathtaking as I drove the car and my eleven-year-old brother cheered me on. With my ego pumped up and the adrenaline rushing, we made our way the mile or so down the familiar country road. I suddenly found myself staring at a covered bridge entrance that I had seen many times before as a passenger that now appeared amazingly narrow in the pitch dark night.

As we passed under the entrance archway, the right side of the car narrowly escaped coming into contact with the old wooden structure. The close proximity between the bridge supports and the automobile in my control suddenly brought great fear to my entire being. This instant sense of fear, most likely God instilled, had made me realize the stupidity of my actions. After safely traversing the bridge, we immediately made a u-turn, cautiously navigated back through the old covered bridge and carefully drove the family station wagon home.

I exercised extreme caution returning the car safely to the garage and made my brother promise to never tell a soul of our short and frightening little jaunt. The fear of God can be quite healthy in situations like these. I eventually shared this experience with my parents in my adulthood many years later. Needless to say, I never attempted to drive my parent's car again prior to turning legal age and receiving my learner's permit. I can only imagine what would have happened to my backside if we had sideswiped the covered bridge that night back in 1979. "Thank God for small miracles!"

The year is 1980, and at fifteen years old I began my sophomore year in a relatively small high school in a relaxed southeastern Pennsylvania community. I thoroughly enjoyed my second year of high school and was somewhat of a popular individual. As an above average student, I was enrolled in college preparatory curriculum and was leaning towards the pursuit of a career in the graphic arts field. Additionally, I was active in many extracurricular activities and also served as the Sophomore Class Vice President.

Athletics played an extremely important role in my development as a well-rounded teenager. In addition to my studies and other activities, I kept rather busy playing three sports: football, basketball and baseball. It was not until many years later that I comprehended the valuable therapeutic effects attributed to my constant involvement in rigorous sporting activities. Most certainly, the high levels of expended energy from my participation in sports had an extremely beneficial effect on my then dormant psychological disorder. The rigid year-round physical exercise and the inner feelings of success it brought undoubtedly stimulated my brain endorphins to maintain my mental health at a fairly even kilter.

Later that year, I began a relationship with a fellow classmate that would eventually have a very profound impact on my life. The attraction for this beautiful tenth-grader grew after a friendship blossomed from having a few school classes together. Melanie Kretzgy was an attractive blond that I had my eyes on for sometime, and upon mustering up the courage to ask her to a school function, I would find out if the attraction I felt was mutual. I was highly enthusiastic after Melanie agreed to accompany me to our high school Christmas dance. Our first date had been scheduled and the butterflies I felt inside me would hopefully dissipate with time. I still remember the evening when I picked her up prior to attending the dance. I nervously waited at her front door, corsage in hand as I stood in the clear, star-filled, cool night air.

After meeting her parents, younger sister and brother, and her curious dog, a pug named Snoopy, we were off to enjoy a festive holiday evening of dancing and innocent school-like romance. Our budding relationship grew quickly as we were able to spend some quality time together on a class trip to Europe over the Christmas - New Year's vacation. The times we shared in Germany and Austria during this trip served as a foundation for what would later become a tale of two high school sweethearts. Within a few months, that pretty, smart and talented blond that had accompanied me to the Christmas dance only months earlier had captured my heart. Melanie was my first true love and she also became my best friend.

March 10, 1981, will be forever etched in my memory as the day my world began to take on a whole new direction. Following a typical school day and after finishing basketball practice, I was waiting in the gym lobby for my mother or father to pick me up for a ride home that evening. When I saw the family car slow to a stop by the curb, I hurried out to catch my ride as I had done many times before. When I opened the door and crawled into the front seat, my heart sank to the pit of my stomach. Something was horribly wrong as I noticed my father, who was normally a quiet and non-emotional man, was crying. At once, I became frightened.

This was the first time I had ever witnessed tears flow from my dad's eyes, and I meekly asked him, "What's wrong?"

He replied in a low, barely audible voice, "Jeff shot himself." Immediately, I became overwhelmed with emotion.

Through my tears I murmured, "Is he okay?"

Dad replied with the answer that I dreaded, "He's dead!"

A life that was so precious to all of us was tragically gone and I was paralyzed with fear for our family as we made the two-and-a-half mile drive home, conducted without another word being spoken. Crying and occasional sniffling were the only sounds that interrupted the eerie silence.

My brother Jeff was the second of four boys and his short life ended that spring day in 1981 at the age of twenty-one. His painful decision to take his life was very traumatic for our entire family and burned a lasting impression deep into my soul. He had always been my closest brother and I loved him very much. Unfortunately, Jeff had become involved in an alcohol and drug abuse lifestyle, self-medicating his mood swings for a few years prior to the culmination of this tragic event. Approximately six months prior to his life ending, he began to spiral out of control. His internal demons began to control his mind taking firm grip of his facilities and convincing him that drugs and alcohol were his only release. Jeff had gotten into trouble with the law for passing some bad checks, and it became blatantly obvious that my big brother needed serious, professional help. That help came in the form of a true "guardian angel" and excellent psychiatrist.

Jeff was hospitalized under the care of the late David E. Nutter, M.D.[2] Dr. Nutter worked tediously with my brother and officially diagnosed him with manic depression, or bipolar disorder as we know it today. Once Jeff's mania was controlled, he was discharged from the hospital and seemed to be doing well in daily outpatient treatment. The legal problems that had arisen during one of his earlier manic ventures had progressed to the stage where it appeared he might have to spend

---

[2] Dr. Nutter passed away September 20, 2004, after battling cancer for many years. His patience and mastery in helping those afflicted with illnesses of the mind was unprecedented.

some time in the county prison. The fear of impending incarceration, relationship problems with his long-time girlfriend and other unknown issues proved to be too much for his psyche, and apparently he felt his only way out of the gloomy darkness was to check out on life.

My mother had been taking Jeff to daily outpatient counseling and support group sessions, as he could not drive himself and had returned to live at home. On that dreary March morning, Jeff insisted on staying at home, missing his therapy and counseling, because he was not feeling well. Mom reluctantly agreed to allow him to stay home, but she had to leave to participate in church activities that had been slated for the day. When she arrived home that afternoon, she went up the stairs to check on him only to find him still in bed. As she called to him with no answer, Mom attempted to awake him only to find his clammy, lifeless body. That experience had to be unbelievably horrifying and I pray that I never have to go through such a terrifying ordeal. Losing a child is one of the most difficult grieving processes, but having to stumble upon your own child's corpse is an unfathomable nightmare. Only an extremely strong and deep spiritually-rooted parent could handle such a devastating experience. God bless her!

As my family, friends and relatives gathered in the living room, emotions spilled over. I cried like I had never done before and the sorrow I felt was unexplainable. "How could he have done this?" I asked myself. In my wildest imagination, I could never envision anyone getting so low and wanting to end their own life. Witnessing the emergency personnel pull the gurney with the body bag by the living room as they headed out the front door and into the waiting ambulance has etched a permanent memory in my mind. The only comfort in this time of extreme grief was the belief that my brother had escaped his "hell on earth" and had left the darkness behind for a brighter, happier place.

The loss of a close family member is quite a devastating experience and for a lengthy period of time, I felt like I was trapped in a very bad dream. Prior to the memorial service for my brother, the funeral director scheduled a private, open casket viewing for just our immediate family. I could not bring myself to participate in this important grieving process. At the age of sixteen, I was unprepared to handle the emotions and fear of seeing my beloved brother lying lifeless in a casket. I did not view his body and later regretted this decision to not take part in such an important act which would have provided closure to a most devastating life event. Jeff's body was cremated and after the memorial service, his ashes were scattered on a close friend's country farm where he had spent many of his happier days on this earth.

For many years after his death, I often dreamed that he had miraculously survived the self-inflicted gunshot wound, and with the help of a mystery neurosurgeon, had made a full recovery and was living in some other part of the country. I never believed these unrealistic dreams, but they continued for quite some time and felt remarkably real and almost believable in my subconscious mind. Reality always sobered me to the fact that he was gone, but in my fantasy world he survived the attempt on his life, and I longed for the day I could see him again. Maybe it was God's way of communicating to me that my brother was indeed alive and well and that I will see him again on the other side of heaven's gate.

My remaining high school years were mostly uneventful except for a few high points. My relationship with Melanie continued to prosper and I remained active in all three sports: football, basketball and baseball. Our baseball team won the league championship in my junior year against insurmountable odds. We had an excellent year but in the final game of the run for the crown, the team fell behind 6-0. After a truly sensational relief pitching effort, some amazing plays and phenomenal clutch hitting, the deficit was overcome and we were victorious by a 7-6 score. Everyone on the team acknowledged some form of divine guidance as we knelt around the pitcher's mound as our coach led us in prayer. I am sure my brother was there to witness our miraculous comeback, and maybe he even had a hand in it?

By the time my senior year arrived, I had become a very popular upperclassman and was quite " a large fish in a small pond," so to speak. Having been elected Senior Class President and continuing to play in all three sports, my life was continually busy. Although the teams I played on were less than stellar, I tried to be a down-to-earth type of person always maintaining an active sense of humor and modesty from my fortunate circumstances. The football team, on which I served as a co-captain, won only one game that fall of 1983, our first contest of the season. A few other games were exciting and close, but despite my valiant efforts to keep the team focused and upbeat, we lost to our remaining nine opponents that season. The highlight of my high school football career came when I was selected to play in the county All Star Game on Thanksgiving Day and our "South" team won by a very comfortable margin. Practicing for a few weeks with many of the best players in the area and being led by a group of exceptional coaches was extremely fun, really rewarding and personally fulfilling. Proud of my spirited play in a challenging contest at that level and winning the annual Thanksgiving Day clash was the icing on the cake to an otherwise dismal senior football season.

Over the winter months, the varsity basketball team was able to win a total of two games, one additional win to that experienced during the fall pigskin season. Fortunately, we were able to play the weakest team in the section twice to record these two wins. The spring of '83 saw our baseball team fair much better as we started out on quite a winning role. After having won the league championship the previous year, although we were under the direction of a new coach, everyone had high expectations. As the season moved forward, our level of play diminished considerably and we finished near .500 for the season.

During my senior year, Melanie and I continued to solidify our youthful relationship as she led the choir of boisterous sideline supporters on the field and on the court as a varsity cheerleader. In addition to our athletic endeavors, both of us served as peer counselors to fellow classmates who sought guidance from someone their own age. After our scholastic activities were through, Melanie and I spent a great deal of our free time together as well. We appeared to be quite the complete couple, and she was a remarkable sweetheart providing needed support constantly, especially during the many discouraging, losing athletic events.

During this last year in high school, my oldest brother Paul and my dad both experienced some behavioral problems and were later diagnosed with bipolar disorder. Sadly, my father had to be put in the hospital to control some increasing bouts of mania that stemmed from current crisis in his life. Dr. Nutter also helped each of them return their lives back to normal. With the help of the medication lithium, both were able to lead active lives experiencing no significant mental health problems. I was extremely thankful and grateful to God that it appeared at that time I was spared this "thorn in the side" that had caused our family many trying times.

In June of 1983, I graduated near the top of my class and many of my friends and I left for the shore after graduation ceremonies to celebrate infamous "Senior Week" in Wildwood, New Jersey. While celebrating our successful completion of high school and enjoying our new-found freedom, the time at the beach was relaxing and fun. As blossoming young adults would be, alcohol played too much of a role that week. At that time in our lives, we were all much too naïve and careless to see the truth of our foolish ways.

One night while intoxicated, I decided to join a few of my friends and headed to the ear-piercing parlor on the boardwalk. I do remember the experience but do not recall any pain whatsoever as I sat still for the parlor attendant as she shot a star-shaped stud through my left ear lobe. I remember walking the boards that night proudly displaying my new ear jewelry, yet feeling like I was in a big bubble from the remaining effects of the alcohol I had consumed earlier that evening. I had convinced myself that getting my ear pierced was "cool" and initially I did enjoy having the earring, but the headache from the hangover was something I could have done without.

After returning from Wildwood, earring and all, the summer after graduation found me working construction to save money to attend college in the fall. I would be attending the Rochester Institute of Technology in Rochester, New York, where I planned to major in Printing Management. Initially I thought it best for Melanie and I to see other people since she would be attending the Massachusetts Institute of Technology in the Boston area, and I would be living in western New York. This decision was pretty much one-sided with me thinking I could break things off cleanly, but I soon realized just how much she meant to me. As the summer progressed, we eventually drifted back together and our relationship seemed strong once again. I will never forget the ride to the Philadelphia International Airport in late August to drop Melanie off to catch a flight to Boston. A new song, "True" by Spandau Ballet, was playing on the radio as we sat in the back seat of her mom's car holding hands, and the words of that song seemed to radiate our every emotion.

Still today, when I hear that song, strong feelings rush back into my mind from that sentimental trip. As Melanie walked onto the plane and

I watched the Air Florida flight taxi away from the gate, I was overcome with emotion. It felt like a part of me died as her mother and I left the terminal. I cried a good portion of the trip home, not truly knowing if I would ever feel whole again. I was a less than perfect boyfriend and I know at times my actions and misaligned ego often hurt Melanie. I sincerely hope she forgave me for my juvenile shortcomings, and to this day, she occupies a very special place in my heart.

CHAPTER THREE
PRELUDE TO AN ILLNESS

Arriving in Rochester, New York, in the fall of 1983 was very exciting and at the same time somewhat overwhelming. The northerly migration from a small high school in rural Pennsylvania where I was a big fish in a very small pond took only five hours. However, upon my arrival at the Rochester Institute of Technology (RIT), it was quickly apparent that I would now be merely a small fish in a vast ocean. Needless to say, this fact came as quite a culture shock to both my psyche and my ego. While working very diligently on my studies and classroom work, my social life was extremely deficient. The only real positive social aspect in my first trimester was during fall tryouts for the RIT men's baseball team. Getting to know many of the returning players was a big plus in my social development, and elation was the mood when I became one of only a few freshman players chosen to play on the varsity squad during the upcoming spring season.

While applying for a job on campus, good old college work-study program, I was introduced to a manager of catering and food services named Gary Gasper. After working in the Clark Dining Hall for a few weeks, Gary and I began to develop a friendship that would grow during my short tenure at RIT and last for many years thereafter. Gary had taken me under his wing and became a very close friend, almost like a brother. He encouraged me to take bartending lessons through the catering division, and eventually I qualified to tend bar at some official Institute events. Gary had run me to the airport in Buffalo a time or two and even took me to see a few Buffalo Sabre hockey games. He introduced me to the home of original "buffalo wings," the Anchor Bar in downtown Buffalo. In the few months I spent at RIT, Gary provided true friendship and genuine concern for a new kid on the block.

We still exchange Christmas cards every year, and I recently flew to Rochester for the evening to visit Gary and have dinner together. Along my life's path and in hindsight, I have been able to identify individuals who I feel were definitely placed in my life to watch over me. Gary was the first of these "guardian angels," and I remain eternally thankful to him for his support and guidance. During my recent visit, I thanked Gary for his guidance that I had received over twenty years ago. He was appreciative of my comments as we attempted to get caught up on lost time while we enjoyed a very stimulating dinner conversation. While discussing many of the past events in our lives, it was apparent that helping others and walking through life "peacefully," trusting in God to be our guiding lights were and remain common paths we both follow.

As my RIT social life continued to fizzle, I began to miss my first love dearly and my heart grew heavy from her absence in my life. It was only under such heartache that I realized just how much she had meant to me. Melanie was my number one confidant and a true emotional lifeline. We spoke from time to time but it was clear that our relationship would not last the test of time. We were able to get together over the Thanksgiving break and discuss our futures. I took it pretty hard, but she felt it best for us to be only friends, because both of our young lives were very stressful and quite demanding, not to mention the distance between us. We agreed to move forward separately and she headed back to New England. I headed back to western New York somewhat dejected and beginning to feel depressed.

After completing the first trimester, my grade point average was a perfect 4.0, but it was obviously apparent I had to slow down and live a little. If I did not learn to enjoy life more and embrace the college experience, I would certainly burn out. I attempted to become more socially active, but the drinking parties and fraternity experiences just were not for me. My emotional well-being began to spiral out of control shortly thereafter. I began to have trouble sleeping and my mind was constantly cluttered with a million thoughts. My concentration ability had become much clouded, thus studying was nearly impossible and my memory was rapidly fading. I had begun to miss home and Melanie was never far from my mind. After a trip to the RIT Infirmary, a classic case of the homesick blues was the diagnosis. I believe the doctor prescribed some medication that I took for a week or so, but my condition failed to improve.

Realizing that any refund on my second trimester tuition could only be exercised till the end of the current week, I made a rash decision to withdraw from RIT effective immediately. After initiating the paperwork at the bursar's office, I called my parents to notify them of my decision to drop out of school and asked them to please come to Rochester to pick up me and my belongings. A few of my professors tried to get me to reconsider my decision and even Gary thought I should hang in there a little longer, but my mind was made up. Shortly before my nineteenth birthday, I was driving back down through the state of New York into Pennsylvania to that friendly place called home. If only I could become the big fish in the small pond again, maybe everything would be fine.

Returning home was initially a big relief, but as the days went by, I began to slip into an expanding darkness. Dropping out of college after achieving a 4.0 was certainly not the norm and when reality set in, I beat myself up mentally and was truly devastated. Furthermore, the friends and girlfriend that had always supplied me with companionship and emotional support were all away at college themselves. As the depression worsened, I began to wish my existence would simply cease. I then knew it was time to get professional help and that's exactly what I did.

My first step was to visit my old high school where I would talk to a very close individual in the guidance office whom I had previously gotten to know quite well. She had mentored the peer counseling program I had been a part of during my years there. Ms. Phillips was very concerned when I broke down emotionally while talking to her and insisted that I contact a very close friend of hers, psychologist Dr. Carolyn Sheaffer. This simple referral was a lifesaving effort, and I have since identified Ms. Phillips as another guardian angel along my life's path. I was told that later in my life (Chapter 8 - The Awakening), I made some valiant efforts to contact her when I was in a semi-psychotic state of mania. God works in mysterious ways, and Ms. Phillips' caring words and compassion steered me in the right direction at a time when I desperately needed it, and for that I am extremely grateful to her.

Dr. Sheaffer saw me for several sessions and we talked about my issues. Her talent and skills along with some anti-anxiety medication eventually allowed the darkness to depart. The sun began to shine again partially helped by a new love I had acquired and by Dr. Sheaffer's insistence that I was not going to end like my brother, which was always a subtle fear that lurked in the back of my mind. So for now, I was once again extremely thankful that I did not have that condition called manic depression or bipolar disorder that had tragically cut short my brother's life nearly three years before. I only had been confronted with a severe case of the blues brought on by situational crisis in my life. As for my new love, the next chapter will explain in detail.

CHAPTER FOUR
FLYING HIGH

As the depression lifted, I began to imagine the new possibilities for my now uncharted future. During my short stay at RIT, while walking to classes over the infamous Quarter Mile,[3] I would often be captivated and inspired by the low flying airliners taking off from Rochester's nearby Monroe County Airport. Dreaming of one day becoming a commercial airline pilot, I had already learned that I was ineligible to receive military flight training because of my inability to meet strict vision requirements without wearing glasses. At that time, it appeared the only way of realizing my dream was to graduate from a prestigious school of higher learning and secure a good job which would eventually allow me to afford the tremendous expense of private flight lessons.

With that option no longer a viable one, I began to investigate the feasibility of pursuing flight instruction at the local community airport. My late uncle, William "Jeff" Jeffries, a retired Air Force officer, was extremely influential and very supportive of my newfound interest.

---

3   The RIT Quarter Mile – a paved pathway between the dormitories and the instructional buildings that all on-campus students had to walk everyday. With some of the inclement weather Rochester experienced, this trek to get to class could be a very challenging adventure.

With Uncle Jeff's encouragement I decided to seriously look into the possibility of learning how to fly, and shortly thereafter my new love for aviation took flight. I was able to fund most of my initial pilot training with the tuition refund from RIT and some personal funds that I had in savings. On March 14, 1984, my first lesson took place. By the time I soloed on April 27th, I realized that I had found an interest, and with some hard work and dedication, it could prosper into a very exciting and rewarding career. I was literally "flying high" and the troubles I had recently experienced seemed like a distant memory.

After receiving my private pilot's license in July of the same year, I began to receive advanced pilot training in pursuit of an instrument flight rating and a commercial pilot's license. Around the same time as I began the advanced pilot training course, I was employed as an aircraft fueler for the same aviation enterprise where I was receiving my flight training. My new employment entitled me to a significant discount on all flight training supplies and even on the expensive flight lessons themselves. In addition to my weekly flight instruction, I enrolled part-time at a local university to continue the pursuit of a college degree as well. Those dark days I had experienced several months before had completely faded away as my new path in life was now clearly charted. This new direction coupled with the excitement of pilot training had revitalized my spirit and motivated me to literally "seek new heights."

Around this time, I began to develop a true friendship with an individual that was also training to become a commercial pilot. Pat Kurtz was from nearby Lebanon County and worked at the Lancaster Municipal Airport as ticket agent for the local commuter airline that flew flights between Lancaster, Pittsburgh, Philadelphia, Baltimore and Kennedy Airport in New York. It is amazing how times have changed. Back then there was service to three or four cities from this small airport, and today only the Pittsburgh service remains, with its longevity seriously in doubt. I first met Pat when he worked as an aircraft fueler for the company where I had been employed. I was hired as the replacement for his soon to be vacated position and his departing responsibility was to provide my initial training. As I got to know Pat better, we began to develop a very special friendship that would last for many years.

Pat was an exceptional airman and also an experienced aerobatic pilot. On several occasions after work, we would rent an aircraft and head out for an evening filled with thrills and excitement. Heading north toward Lebanon, we would fly over his parent's house at low altitude and shout to his family below as one of us cut the engine back so the noise of the small plane would be reduced to a low murmur. At times, we would head to a nearby small airport and accomplish accuracy and short field landing competitions. While coming in too low on one approach to the uncontrolled runway, I accidentally snared the thorn bushes on the bank prior to the landing surface. Like a fighter jet catching the cable on the flight deck of an aircraft carrier, we came to a very short stop. That landing was the shortest ever, but great care was taken to ensure that this type of landing never occurred again. I was very thankful that the small aircraft sustained no damage from my short field stunt. A few times, Pat would rent an aerobatic plane, and with our parachutes on, we would head out for some truly upside down excitement. Two nineteen-year-olds having the time of our lives while buzzing around the skies of south central Pennsylvania was a real blast.

With this new love for aviation, I practically lived, ate and slept piloting for the longest time. My desire to be successful in this new endeavor created a drive in me like I had never known before. After a lot of persistence and hard work, a little over a year from the start of my flight training, I had received all the ratings and certificates required by the Federal Aviation Administration to allow me to work for hire as a pilot. Furthermore, I received a Certified Flight Instructor license which provided an avenue for me to begin working as a flight instructor. Most all new pilots have to spend time instructing, building hours, in order to be attractive applicants for any gainful employment, such as flying for a corporation or eventually landing a commercial airline piloting position.

My time was now split between work as an aircraft fueler, part-time flight instructing and attending evening courses at the local university. I had now logged nearly five hundred flight hours and the biggest opportunity of my budding career was about to happen. Having done all my flight training at the place where I was currently working allowed me to impress the chief pilot, who also held the title of Federal Aviation Administration designated examiner, with my above average piloting skills and exceptional flying ability. Although my experience was somewhat limited, my qualities as an outstanding individual and of a talented commercial pilot were duly noted.

One summer day in 1985, while studying my college coursework in the fuel truck that had become like a second home during my work week, my pager went off. It was the chief pilot, Ad, and he summoned me to his office, as soon as possible. When I arrived at his office a few moments later, the biggest break of my aviation life was thrust upon me. I stared at Ad in total disbelief as he explained that one of the full-time charter pilots had suddenly resigned his position and that he was promoting me to the charter department to act as a first officer on the company's King Air.[4] I was needed to serve as co-pilot on a three-day trip scheduled to depart that afternoon.

As I drove home to shower and pack, the euphoria was nearly uncontrollable. Was this opportunity really unfolding right before my

---

[4] A King Air is a medium sized turbo-prop airplane manufactured by Beech Craft (now Raytheon) and is capable of transporting six-ten people in business-like comfort.

eyes or was I stuck in a dream that I had envisioned might someday come true. Upon my return to the airport, it was highly apparent that I was not dreaming as the chief pilot and I taxied out in King Air "N721K" for my short introductory check out in this beautiful aircraft that I had only dreamed of flying just hours before. Ad and I flew the King Air around the airport traffic pattern a few times, practicing takeoffs and landings. After I received my abbreviated check out in the King Air C90 aircraft, I then learned the specifics of the southbound trip.

A short time later Mike, the aircraft's captain, and I were rolling down Runway 31, gently lifting off the pavement and climbing to an altitude that was higher than I had ever been before, heading in the direction of Greensboro, North Carolina. I barely had time to reflect on this truly amazing day and my promotion from aviation fueler to King Air co-pilot. As we leveled off at 20,000 feet, I truly felt like I was in heaven. This astounding career advancement would not have been possible without the confidence and dependability Ad placed in me. All the respect in the world goes out to him for giving me a "once in a lifetime opportunity." For this remarkable career opportunity, I am forever thankful to my first Chief Pilot, the late Adam Mattern.

My career advanced quite nicely after reaching this new plateau. After a full year of flying co-pilot on the King Air and as a charter pilot on some of the company's other aircraft, I decided to accept an employment opportunity with a charter company out of Reading, Pennsylvania. Serving as a pilot for this new company would allow me to fly larger, newer aircraft, but more importantly would allow me to fly more hours and help me accumulate time faster in my ultimate pursuit of a commercial airline career. In my few years of corporate and charter flying experiences, I was able to travel to many interesting destinations and hence enjoyed meeting many unique individuals.

The highlights of my travels included trips to Orlando, Florida, Gulf Shores and Tuscaloosa, Alabama (Crimson Tide football games), Nantucket, Massachusetts and South Bend, Indiana (Notre Dame football games). I had the opportunity to fly many corporate executives as well as some notable politicians and sport celebrities, such as former U.S. Congressman Jack Kemp, former Pennsylvania Governor Richard Thornburg, former Major League catcher Johnny Bench and Penn State's legendary Joe Paterno to name a few. During my charter piloting years, most of my experiences were enjoyable and I liked my job for the most part.

On August 2, 1986, I met a beautiful young lady named Andrea Striker. Michael Birch, my God brother, had invited me over to his apartment to have pizza and watch some basketball on television. I was to meet him at the mall where he managed a retail shoe store. After he had closed the store, we would then head back to his place. That evening, unbeknown to me, he had met an old girlfriend while working and had asked her and her friend, Andrea, to hang around until the mall closed so that the two of them could join us for some pizza and entertainment. I had no idea that I was being set up, but fortunately this blind date went pretty well.

I arrived after the mall was closed and while waiting for Mike to exit the store, two young ladies approached and asked me, "Are you Al?" When I answered that I was they responded, " We are here to get you!" Wow, what a cool and flattering experience, two beautiful young women sent to "get me." The night went better than can be expected for Andrea and myself with both of us not knowing that we were in for this chance encounter. After the evening drew to a close, I asked this beautiful brunette with an air of innocence if she would consider going out again and she stated that she would indeed. As our relationship began to grow, I slowly began to realize the joys of having a true love back in my life again.

That same year, while at my parents' home, my darling Andrea and I were sitting at the table eating Thanksgiving dinner when my pager went off. After calling work, I would have to leave immediately for the airport to fly to Philadelphia to pick up an important piece of machinery which had to be flown to an oil refinery in Corpus Christie, Texas. After spending my Thanksgiving Day in an airplane, without my loved ones, it was apparent that the airline career that I had always longed for would offer significant scheduling benefits to our budding romance. It was obvious what had to be done, so I began an aggressive pursuit of an airline piloting position.

In August of 1987, I started my airline career with a small commuter airline based in Allentown, Pennsylvania. My good friend Pat had earned a pilot position with the same regional airline company after working for a few years as a ticket agent and also as a King Air co-pilot in the airline's charter flight department. After completing training, I was based in Reading and spent most of my free time with my new love Andrea. Additionally, I was enrolled part-time at the Pennsylvania State University – Berks Campus where I was pursuing an associate's degree in Business Administration. Making financial ends meet was extremely difficult on a first year salary of only $11,400 which included no provisions for overtime.

Contrary to public opinion, new pilot pay in the commuter airline industry was not the glamorous job many made it out to be. I was able to moonlight on the side for a few local corporations to help pay my bills, and eventually I moved back with my parents to support my flying habit. Later that year on Christmas day before I had to leave for work, I asked the charming and cute Andrea to marry me. She said, "Yes!" Our engagement lasted for nearly eighteen months as I continued to build valuable flight time at the local commuter airline, and Andrea enrolled in business school in pursuit of a degree in Computer Information Systems. We set a wedding date in May of 1989 which would give us plenty of time to plan for the big day.

I remember vividly back to the first day Pat and I flew together in the cockpit of our carrier's regional airliner. What an amazing experience and ecstatic feeling! Remembering our thrill seeking and "barnstormer" flying just a few years earlier, we were now entrusted with the lives of the thirty-some passengers in the back of this small commuter aircraft. Pat had just been upgraded to the position of Captain, and I had the honor of flying with him on his first trip after completing his operating experience training. Between the two of us, there was a total of forty-six years on the flight deck, not years of experience, but total years (simply twenty-three times two). Although our youth was evident, our skill as pilots and dedication to safety made for quite a complete and thorough flight crew. He was an extremely competent Captain and I was a very experienced First Officer and we made a great team while flying together.

Later, I learned that Pat was going through some very trying emotional times in his own life and was having great difficulty sleeping. My being there as both a professional pilot and a close friend helped ease some of the anxiety he was feeling from his enlarged responsibilities as Captain. He went through some "hellish" personal experiences earlier in life relating to an improper relationship with a Catholic priest at his local parish. Pat was able to persevere through the struggles and mental anguish by holding on to his deep faith in God. I am glad I was there for him in his time of need, as he would eventually be there for me as the future would reveal my fate farther down the road of life.

After a year and a half had passed since I began employment with my first airline, the working environment became very hostile as the management and the pilots' union had become entangled in a bitter labor dispute. Pat was able to secure a flight officer position with a highly respected airline in the Midwestern United States. I began to get very disgruntled with my current piloting job and aggressively pursued employment with a major airline or a more attractive regional carrier. In the spring of 1989, I accepted a flight officer position with one of the best airlines in the industry headquartered in Appleton, Wisconsin, the same airline that Pat had joined several months earlier. I was truly excited about this great opportunity with one of the country's premier airlines and was encouraged by the much improved financial compensation package. Pat and I joked about his futile efforts to move on to bigger and better opportunities, seemingly always having me follow behind, following the same career paths once again.

After completing initial training for this new job, I was based in Richmond, Virginia, and commuted back and forth to central Pennsylvania for a few months until Andrea completed her computer information systems degree and our wedding was behind us. Pat and I shared an apartment close to the airport while I made the commute home during my days off to spend time with my bride to be. I will never forget Pat's fail-safe, redundant wake up system. As airline pilots, we would at times have to awake during the very early morning hours. The possibility of oversleeping and missing a trip was frightening to a new flight officer. Pat always set three alarm clocks: One was electric, another was battery operated and the third was an old wind up type. When all three alarms went off, sometimes simultaneously, the entire apartment would fill with buzzing, ringing and mind-jarring clanging to ensure he did not oversleep. Needless to say, Pat never missed a wake up call.

My new employer was caring and generous in allowing me ample time off to prepare for my upcoming wedding. On May 6, 1989,

Andrea and I were married in an old historic Church with family and friends present. After a short yet enjoyable honeymoon in Cancun, Mexico, we relocated to our first apartment home on the east side of Richmond. We rented a small one bedroom apartment, just down the street from Pat and his new wife Kristina's place. The four of us spent a good deal of time together and remained close friends for some time. After Andrea located employment in the Richmond area, we began to save our money and dreamed of eventually owning a home.

After six months of living on the east side, we decided to move to the west side of Richmond, actually following Pat and Kristina to a more upscale place called Champions Pointe Apartments and Athletic Club. After six months in this new apartment, we were able to purchase our first home also on the west side near Glen Allen, Virginia. Our new house was a small three-bedroom rancher with white siding and a black shingle roof. The best attribute of our new home was a wooden front porch that contained a cute country swing that Andrea and I enjoyed relaxing on. My career had progressed quite nicely and my salary finally increased to a level that we could begin to enjoy life a little more. Our friends, Pat and Kristina had purchased a home as well and learned that they were expecting a baby. Andrea and I were very happy and began to think about starting a family of our own.

CHAPTER FIVE
NETWORK MARKETING MIRAGE

About the time we were beginning to think of the Richmond area as our home and had nearly adjusted to being Southerners, a difficult adjustment for Yankees at heart, Andrea was no longer satisfied with her original job at a large Virginia-based life insurance company. Attempting to find a new employer, she interviewed with an independent head-hunter for a position advertised in the local newspaper. Some time after successfully landing another position, Andrea received a call from a man named Arthur Hedrick, identifying himself only as a network marketer. He explained that he had received her name from the head-hunter, who was later determined to be his wife, and wanted to meet with Andrea to discuss an opportunity with his own marketing firm. Andrea reluctantly agreed to meet this marketing "President," but she reasoned that perhaps he would provide a better employment position than the one she had recently started.

Andrea met him at a local fast food restaurant where he attempted to describe a tremendous income-producing venture to her. When she returned from the meeting, she was not really sure what to think. From the brief appointment and his vague descriptions, she thought it was something involving sales and marketing of products and services.

Then, he invited both of us to a more formal presentation at a hotel meeting site on the south side of town. Andrea and I were not really interested, and she was highly skeptical of his bigger-than-life sales pitch. After several follow-up phone calls, this so-called president of an international marketing company continued to request our presence at another of his informational meetings. I had often envisioned being in business for myself and something about the concept was appealing to me, so after many refusals we finally decided to attend this business opportunity seminar held at a hotel in the Midlothian, Virginia, area.

The business opportunity meeting was very informational and designed to heighten our interest levels further. The presenter, a prominent dentist who had been able to replace his own professional income in a very short time after entering this business, illustrated how a family could make significant amounts of money with just a minimal amount of time commitment. It sounded too good to be true, but I was a believer in hard-working attitudes and thought with dedication and effort, if this guy could do it, so why couldn't I? I was initially very excited! Andrea remained somewhat skeptical and in retrospect, I believe she saw the big "sales job" that I failed to see. After sitting through nearly an hour of this highly professional presentation, we were told that the network marketing plan being introduced to us was pulled together by a well-known Fortune 500 company, the Amway Corporation.

This chapter is not meant to judge any individual for wrong doing, only God can make that determination. However, it will explore areas in the Amway organization which relate to the overall culture and drive behind this powerful marketing establishment. One must first understand that Amway is a sales organization, and the sales and marketing plan it offers looks in the beginning to be quite attractive. In essence, money can be made not only on products one sells, but additionally on override percentages of all sales volume created in an individual's network of distributors. For those not familiar with the Amway world, the sales and marketing plan is a "pyramid-like" system, where the money always flows to the top. To date, it is legal; however, this section of the book attempts to shed light into the areas of ethics, morals and cult-like manipulation that had a very profound effect on my life. Again, I want to reassure all readers that this chapter is written not to condemn the organization or judge individuals, but simply to relate my real-life Amway network marketing experiences.

Amway is comprised of millions of independent distributors who market many fine products and services. The Amway Corporation itself is an outstanding company and an honorable environmental neighbor. The company's world headquarters and principle business operations are located in Ada, Michigan. If only more companies in America adopted their business philosophies, the world would certainly be a nicer place for all of us to live. The focus of my experiences in this chapter will be on a particular division within Amway known as the "Britt Organization"[5] named after its spiritual leader and original entrepreneur Mr. William "Bill" Britt.

The marketing ideas presented at the business orientation meeting seemed to make some sense even with all the hype. It was made apparent to newcomers that by purchasing goods and services in mass quantity, eliminating the middleman, individual consumers could save a considerable amount of money. After lengthy discussions and careful consideration, Andrea and I decided to join the Amway network hoping to save some money by utilizing a large marketing organization as a wholesale buying club.

---

[5] A separate and distinct division within Amway that has been featured on the CBS News documentary 60 Minutes™ for its highly questionable marketing tactics.

As we purchased products on a regular basis, the marketer that brought us into the organization, now known as our "sponsor," had become an integral part of our lives. He and his wife were seemingly cordial and often went out of their way to build a friendship on the common ground of our business association. The four of us grew into what appeared to be a genuine friendship, but business which meant making money through Amway, and constant motivational encouragement with respect to the business aspects eventually created a very one-dimensional relationship. Our sponsor provided motivational tapes which encouraged our increased participation in the network marketing organization. These tapes were designed in a manner that played very highly on one's emotions. I was the only one that listened to the tapes as Andrea was still not sold on the whole idea. My somewhat obsessive-type personality and drive toward perfection began to crave this highly idealistic information. A real personality metamorphosis began to occur as I became more and more wrapped up in this huge cult-like atmosphere.

Our sponsor encouraged our participation in an event which was called "Dream Weekend," a weekend that was billed as an experience that would change your life and the way you viewed all things. Initially, both Andrea and I were not the least bit interested in attending this out-of-town event. After what seemed to be borderline badgering by our sponsor, we decided to give the much touted weekend event an open-minded try. Our sponsor was absolutely right, that weekend in Baltimore, Maryland, started a fire inside me that would change my life forever – only in a very negative and potentially damaging way.

During this weekend of business meetings, seminars and a pep rally, the event was characterized by an excitement which I had never seen before in my life. People were literally going crazy about the prospects of the Amway business, and hooting and hollering were commonplace.

This atmosphere of excitement and vigor was certainly contagious and I caught the bug early. The energy levels experienced within the confines of the hotel convention center was truly electrifying, causing me to view the many successful people in this organization who spoke that weekend as if they were almost idyllic super humans. Surely, I could accomplish what others had done and be just as successful, if not better, than these folks, were the thoughts going through my rather absorbed mind.

Then, Sunday morning came. That morning's activities would be a day I will never forget for as long as I walk upon this earth. It began the transformation of my soul from a happy God-loving person to an inadequate, guilt-ridden God-fearing sinner. Mr. Bill Britt, the self-proclaimed leader of this powerful arm within Amway, delivered a very emotional message that pulled hard at my heart strings. He spoke of how many individuals will be surprised on the day of reckoning (the rapture) when many of us thinking we were saved Christians would be viewed as useless sinners spit out by God to face the wraths of heathen men. His fire-charged words literally seemed to hypnotize and captivate my soul, scaring the living hell out of me. After his sermon, I was convinced beyond any reasonable doubt that I had to be a "model" Christian to go anywhere successfully in life. Also as a result of Mr. Britt's reckless preaching, I instinctively began to plan the drastic changes in my lifestyle that would be necessary if I wanted to obtain my ticket to heaven upon the end of my earthly existence. A man whom I had never met before this day with his diamond rings, a carefully staged presentation of great wealth and the perceived power of a Godly messenger sent my heart and soul into an eventual state of wandering that would last nearly two years.

I learned that Bill Britt believed he was a prophet of God, and after hearing his "fire and brimstone" preaching style, at that point in time I viewed him as such. Reform and change on my part were most

41

definitely in order to have any hope of my success in this short life and to eventually make the leap to something better beyond this earthly realm. Thus, the ties between Amway and my Christian character were forged into one that Sunday morning. I was brainwashed into thinking that this was God's direction for me. Unfortunately, I even felt like it was the only path in which I must succeed or be doomed to a lifetime of failures. The Britt organization's dependence on and association with Christianity created a very dangerous cult-like atmosphere for individuals who took their religious beliefs seriously. Unfortunately, I was one of these vulnerable individuals.

In hindsight, I should have been able to separate the truth from the smoke clouds Mr. Britt had created, but I was so caught up in the emotion of the weekend that the lines between reality and this fantasy world were not distinguishable. One infamous reference I have hung onto all these years occurred during that Sunday morning "church" service. Bill Britt proclaimed that the beauty of the Amway business was as follows: "You only have to be like Jesus. Find twelve leaders and teach them to recruit new followers and you will create a great business built on the solidest of all foundations, the Rock." I was always taught and still believe to this day that the son of God taught his disciples to be " Fishers of Men."[6] His loyal followers were told to preach the message of salvation and to communicate faith, hope and love to all humanity, not to create power and wealth for certain organizational elite.

When we arrived home after that weekend in Maryland, my efforts to lead this new life that I had perceived to be a calling from God turned my entire world upside down. The daily things that I once enjoyed doing were now believed as improper use of my limited, valuable time. I no longer read the paper, watched the news or any TV that was

---

[6]   "And He saith onto them, follow Me and I shall make you fishers of men." Matthew 4:19

perceived to be destructive to the soul. Even sports seemed no longer important even though watching and playing sports had always played a big role in my life and had previously brought a significant amount of enjoyment to me. The experience of living, sleeping and eating Amway, my new direction in life, created an overwhelming amount of anxiety and constant unrest. Unending worry of success surrounded my life, my career and my marriage, and began to zap any sense of peace and fulfillment that life had to offer. It was not long before all of this worry and anxiety began to take a major toll on my body's mental and physical capabilities as well. I was beginning to have trouble sleeping at night with all my mind's preoccupations with Amway, and I could only pray to God to see me through.

Chapter Six
Dawn of the Darkness

With my continuing high levels of worry and anxiety, I began to experience serious difficulty sleeping. While out of town on a three-day flying assignment, Andrea called me in my overnight hotel to share some exciting news. After trying to start a family for nearly six months, she was unable to contain her excitement and could not wait until I returned from my trip to let me know that the home pregnancy test showed positive results. We were going to be parents. At first I was extremely happy, upbeat and looking forward to being a father, but soon the many sleepless nights had begun to wear down my mental capacities and played tricks on my mind. The added anxiety of knowing a small child would soon be entering our lives coupled with the parenting responsibilities which lay ahead in my marriage and the continuing obsessive, intrusive thoughts of the Amway business venture I had been pursuing were taxing my brain beyond reasonable limits. At this point, it was obvious to me that professional medical attention was needed for my deteriorating mental condition and worsening insomnia.

Upon returning to Richmond later that week, I immediately scheduled an appointment with my family physician to have my health evaluated. Dr. Ken Sampson was very concerned about my high anxiety levels when I explained how I was literally sleeping only a few hours each night. Informing me that he had seen these symptoms in other new expectant parents many times, he assured me that with some time the growing anxiety would taper off and eventually go away. In his opinion he felt my condition did not warrant any specialized psychiatric treatment or psychological counseling at this time. Up to now, my mood had remained fairly positive; however, my lack of sleep was slowly pushing me toward a distant darkness. With his strong Christian beliefs and holistic medical views, Dr. Sampson encouraged me to relax and pray for God to lift the burden of the massive amounts of anxiety I had piled into my life. His insistence on a Godly healing process through prayer routed in his deep faith was very much appreciated at the time and seemed like a logical solution. However, in retrospect, my strong family history of depression and bipolar disorder was severely discounted, and his "faith healing" approach to a possible more severe diagnosis was somewhat misguided.

He assured me that the marvelous power of the Lord and the Holy Spirit could rectify my condition if I faithfully believed in His healing power. I wholeheartedly believed this spiritual encouragement I was given by my family medical physician, and began to pray fervently making repeated pleas to the Man above for deliverance from my anxieties and sleeplessness that had gripped my life. With almost continual prayer and total belief in the healing touch of an all powerful, all knowing God, I became very discouraged when after several days my condition showed no improvement. After all that I had been through, I now seriously began questioning the level of my faith. As no relief came, my thoughts were that God was not curing me of my worsening symptoms because something was not right in my relationship with Him, just as that prophetic Amway leader had preached to my fearful soul some months earlier. Dr. Sampson's holistic approach to my mental health issues further cultivated the "seeds of guilt" that sent me deeper into a soul searching nightmare. I asked myself, "Why would a loving and caring God whom I had always known and worshipped punish me in such a way?" My spiritual self being was sent into a dangerous tailspin, and this feeling of inadequacy in God's eye created a massive barrier to overcome in the tough emotional fight that would lie ahead.

In addition to large dosages of prayer, I had made a commitment to get much more exercise than I had gotten regularly for some time. Strenuous physical activity would be helpful to my condition by causing the brain's natural ability to produce endorphins to be maximized. This increased brain chemistry would hopefully help the neurotransmitters of my mind calm down at night allowing me to feel tired and possibly get some much needed sleep. When at home on my days off from work, I would ride my bike for many miles everyday and do repetitious exercises, like sit ups and push ups, in an attempt to tire my body and mind out. When away on a flying trip, I would spend several hours jogging and exercising before or after my flight duties were complete for the day. I also tried taking nutritional supplements and extracts designed to calm the mind such as valerian root, chamomile tea, to name a few, and even drinking a warm glass of milk prior to bedtime each night. Despite my continuously earnest prayers, a rigid exercise routine and a supplement regimen designed to dull my over active mind, I was still having great difficulty getting adequate rest. My body weight was down to levels I had not seen since my teenage years, and my pilot uniform became excessively baggy as many of my co-workers became increasingly concerned for my health. Not sleeping during the night causes one's metabolism to work overtime, and I was beginning to grow terribly thin and looked quite frail.

Needless to say, my alertness in the cockpit was severely diminished as my condition continued to worsen. Still flying as a First Officer or second-in-command, I was able to disguise my degrading performance to some extent. Having recently been awarded a Captain position on a new aircraft we would be receiving, I was expected to attend initial training in Toronto, Canada at the beginning of August. My lack of mental attentiveness and an increasing inability to concentrate would make successful completion of this upcoming training nearly impossible. After a week or two of flying in this somewhat lethargic state, I knew that I would have to hang up my pilot hat for awhile to address my deteriorating condition. I vividly remember my last leg in the cockpit of an airliner as I made the southerly flight between Washington Dulles and Richmond's Byrd Airports. It was my leg to fly and as I rolled the aircraft onto final approach to Runway 20, my emotions took over as the tears began to fall from my weary eyes. Upon landing in Richmond, I would advise the domicile flight manager of my inability to attend training in Canada and my need for a leave of absence for medical reasons. As the Fokker aircraft settled to the runway, the touchdown was perhaps one of the smoothest I have ever accomplished. Knowing that I would not get many more landing chances for some time, I found it quite fitting that I "greased it on." Little did I know at that time, this emotional touchdown would be the last actual landing of a large airliner of my career.

Later that day, I scheduled an emergency appointment with Dr. Sampson. After trying to beat the symptoms I had been plagued with for several weeks, we both agreed it best for me to take a medical leave of absence from my piloting career until my sleep patterns returned to normal. After writing the letter and officially taking me off flight duty until further notice, he also referred me to a local Christian counseling service where I would attend some much needed therapy sessions to help with my situation in an attempt to try and ease my anxieties and remedy my sleeplessness. Brian Burton was the counselor's name to whom Dr.

Sampson referred me, and his efforts were excellent right from the start, assuring me that I would make it through these difficult times. At that point I was starting to feel some serious blues as the early stages of depression began to set in. After a few sessions, Brian's shrewd skills as a counselor recognized that my symptoms and condition appeared to be more than just some minor, anxiety-induced emotional problems. He recommended that I also see a psychiatrist to explore the possibility of a chemical imbalance leading to my sleeplessness and growing depression. Brian recommended a fellow Christian psychiatrist named Dr. Martin Hoffer.

After my first visit to Dr. Hoffer, he definitely concurred with Brian and prescribed the anti-depressant medication, Imipramine, to treat me for an official diagnosis of "Major Depression." As I formulated my initial impressions of Dr. Hoffer, I must say this pudgy-faced, bearded, psychiatrist did not overwhelmingly impress me. His somewhat strange mannerisms, marginally effective techniques and awkward communication delivery felt rather odd to my highly professional personality. However, at this point I was pretty emotionally distraught and was desperate for help in any way, shape or form that relief was offered. I was comfortable with Brian and thought highly of his counseling skills. Dr. Hoffer was recommended by him, hence I certainly thought it had to be a good thing, and it was extremely important to me to have my psychiatric doctor to be rooted in the Christian faith as well. The seriousness of my condition increased significantly with the realization that medicine had been prescribed and an official diagnosis of depression attached to my medical history. Having to go on prescribed psychotropic medication was a huge disappointment, since I realized the devastating effect this particular medication would have on my still young aviating career.

After returning home that afternoon and speaking with my pilot's union medical counsel, I was told that I could expect to be out of work for six to twelve months, possibly longer. This news only seemed to intensify the anxiety to an overwhelming level, and I remember vividly that day when I was on the phone with Dr. Stark from the aeromedical office in Denver, Colorado. I was pretty upset as he explained that I would not be allowed to return to my career for quite some time and the possibility existed that I might never return. I was overwhelmed with irrational fear and panic set in as I searched feverishly through my life insurance policies. I had attempted to see what benefits my wife and child on the way would be able to collect if I decided to "check out early" in life. I learned that suicide clauses in many of my policies would make death benefits null and void if I chose to exercise this selfish option in my time of deep desperation. Over the next few weeks, matters were made worse when the prescribed medication had not worked as planned, and I was no better off over a month into treatment for my unresponsive depression.

After being off work for a few weeks, I decided to search for some part-time employment to supplement our income as we prepared to ready our home for the child expected in February of 1992. Locating part-time work would also allow me to get out of the house regularly and attempt to get my mind off the worries and fears that often strangled any ability I might have to experience pleasure and joy. I interviewed for and was offered a position working as a men's suit salesman at a local mall for a newly designed franchise named Tailor's Row. The individuals with whom I worked, Ed, Bill, Sandy and Eddie, were friendly and supportive of me. Their temporary encouragement and friendship was therapeutic in nature and helped me weather some very difficult times. The position itself was fairly unrewarding, but the job generated some income and gave me valuable contact with positive people at a time when I desperately needed it.

My other part-time job was as a pizza delivery driver for a national pizza chain. The income from my delivery work was somewhat substantial and including gratuities I was able to make more money driving and delivering pizzas around the countryside than I did in my suit and tie retail job at the mall. Furthermore, free food was an added benefit as many nights I could take home a pizza or two that were made in error and would otherwise have been thrown out. This initially "cool" fringe benefit lost its appeal quickly after eating pizza repeatedly a few nights in a row. Talking to all the employees and managers back at the store between delivery assignments was a lot of fun, and I valued the independence while on the road making my deliveries. I would listen to music from the radio and my cassette tape player while making my rounds and found the experience positive and quite uplifting. A few downsides of this delivery position were first, every once in a while you would not receive a tip, which those of us in the trade called getting "stiffed." Secondly, was that my car began to smell after having acquired a distinct pizza-smelling aroma.

Another positive influence during these very trying times was the relationship Andrea and I had with many friends through our church family. We were members of the Mechanicsville United Methodist Church, and the love and support we received from our preacher and the congregation served as a remarkable lifeline. Pastor Graham Bamberger, a very rigid yet caring minister, was another true "guardian angel," ministering to my wounded soul throughout my mental health ordeal while we lived in the Richmond area. Graham met with me on several occasions, helping me navigate through the valleys of darkness and clarified the misconceptions of my overwhelming feelings of inadequacy in God's eyes. I am also thankful for the many friends that were there for us in our most trying of times, especially Deborah and Robert Horn. They always showed great concern for us, and our short lived friendship before moving away from the area was truly a blessing from God.

One other tremendously supportive family helpful during my time of despair was the Bishops. I had purchased a used car from their family business shortly after arriving to central Virginia and a wonderful friendship grew over time. Melvin, Bliss and Debbie were truly special people, and I will be forever indebted to them for their caring and generous souls. Melvin was a powerful Christian man and did some amazing preaching to me, lifting my spirits when I needed it the most. He took me fishing on several occasions and allowed me to work in his auto repair shop to pocket some needed money during my initial time off from flying. More importantly than the financial compensation from knowing him, was the positive enforcement I received every day and the uplifting of my soul from this kindest of men and his family. A few years ago, I learned that Bliss and Melvin's beloved daughter Debbie had passed away due to complications from multiple sclerosis. May her soul rest high in that most majestic of places – heaven!

I was still having great difficulty receiving adequate rest at night and struggled daily to stay out of the emotional cellar. Dr. Hoffer and I realized that the initial medication prescribed for my depressive symptoms was not accomplishing its intended purpose. He chose to change my medication to something more progressive. The modern anti-depressant Prozac was substituted for my initial medication and some heavy tranquilizers were also prescribed. The sleeping pills, Halcyon, would be used as needed in an attempt to increase my ability to fall asleep and obtain a quality night's rest. Physically I was exhausted from the continued lack of sleep and mentally I was worn out. I knew that the medication needed some time to "kick in," but I was experiencing zero relief and the continuing darkness began to grow darker each day. I often would severely struggle just to get out of bed and to grab a shower before my wife was scheduled to arrive home from work so that she would not know the level of my growing depression.

The gripping depression grew deeper and deeper and the expanding darkness began to impact every facet of my life. The smothering symptoms and accompanying hopelessness were nearly paralyzing as the depths of the despair increased to unexplainable levels. I now began to think that the only escape from the engulfing darkness was to take my own life, thus ending the pain and suffering. When my brother Jeff ended his earthly existence some ten years earlier, I was completely unable to fathom the possibility of how anyone's mindset could slump so low that they would feel suicide to be a viable alternative. As my fight to live teetered on a very delicate balance, I then realized that it was quite possible! My planned demise was never far from my mind as I would try to formulate how and when. Fortunately, my destructive thoughts would be interrupted by images of my beloved wife and our child to be. I would attempt to focus my attention on planning a way to end my existence in a non-gruesome manner, but each time when I thought of Andrea and the baby in her womb, I would slowly back away from the edge of that very dangerous cliff. Another line of reasoning that kept me from acting on my destructive intentions was that I realized God was the giver of all life and I was not authorized to snuff out any life, including my own. If, I thought, I carried out these plans to end my existence, certainly God would condemn me for my final cowardly act. Only He could choose to have me "check out" of this world, so I had to persevere.

Just a few hundred yards from our home was a major train intersection that saw activity pretty much twenty-four hours a day. When we first moved in, the blaring train whistles in the middle of the night were quite disturbing, Over time, we became accustomed to the nighttime tones of the freight and passenger trains that rambled through our neighborhood. Lying on the busy train tracks during one of my sleepless nights was one of the plans I had envisioned for ending my pain and hopelessness. Swerving my bike into the path of an oncoming truck during one of my many bike rides or pointing my deer rifle to my head and mustering up the courage to pull the trigger were a few additional acts I had contemplated. The continuing ability to control my overwhelming thoughts of despair and self-destruction was growing thinner every minute of every day.

One afternoon, while lying in bed the entire day, I came extremely close to swallowing an entire bottle of my prescribed sleeping medication. It was at that moment that I realized I could no longer trust my ebbing and waning thoughts of suicide. The line between maintaining control and ending the unbearable pain all but withered away in the deadly darkness. With the ability to guarantee my physical safety no longer possible, hospitalization would be a necessity if I were to continue to persevere the "slings and arrows" of the now potentially disastrous major depressive episode.

After telling my counselor, Brian, the scope of my destructive thoughts, he pushed to have me immediately admitted to a psychiatric hospital. I begged him to allow me a few days to prepare for my institutionalization, because our families had planned a baby shower for Andrea back in Pennsylvania during the upcoming weekend. Although my condition was quite fragile, I did not want her to know the severity of my situation until after her special event had taken place. Brian was extremely hesitant to allow me to go, but if I would promise not to do any harm to myself, he would allow me to take the short trip north. My promise was given.

That weekend at Andrea's parents' home was undoubtedly one of the biggest emotional roller coaster rides of my entire life. More profoundly was the devastating ride for my expectant wife. Immediately after her baby shower, when all the guests had left the house, I struggled through the tears and broke the news to Andrea, her parents and my parents that I would be checking myself into the hospital first thing Monday morning upon our arrival back in the Richmond area. My parents and in-laws seemed to understand my grief and were very supportive of this critical decision. However, my dear wife Andrea was crushed at the news and appeared heartbroken. As we drove back to Virginia that Sunday evening, the tension in our vehicle was unbearable. I felt some emotional relief due to getting through the weekend festivities, but the reality of my situation was still rather sobering. By letting everyone know the severity of my condition, the truth had been told and my spirits again began to sink into the unfathomable depths of darkness as the miles passed on the highway home. Only God knew what was going through Andrea's mind as we made that lonely journey southward to our Glen Allen, Virginia, residence.

The very next morning, my loving wife drove me to the psychiatric hospital to be admitted for inpatient treatment. Andrea appeared very strong, supportive and somewhat rejuvenated following the weekend's wild emotional roller coaster ride. The admission process took a few hours and then with some emotional tears being shed, it was time to say "goodbye" to my wife. I can only imagine what sorrow Andrea felt as she drove home alone that afternoon, now almost eight months pregnant. Many angels from heaven above certainly accompanied her on the ride home and provided strength and comfort to her through these very trying times she was forced to endure.

As I settled into my new surroundings, the staff went through my personal belongings to be certain I had nothing in my possession that could be used to harm myself. They took my razor as well as a compact mirror and a glass container of after shave lotion that I had in my travel kit. I was given a bed in a semi-private room shared with my new roommate, Jerry. Jerry was a middle-aged African-American who worked for the local railroad as a brakeman and was trying to recover from a bout of serious depression also. He and I got along considerably well, but we both often spent too much time in bed trying to sleep away the blues that we just couldn't seem to shake. In his better moods and during lighter moments, Jerry was extremely witty and quite jovial as well. His speech patterns and mannerisms often reminded me of the actor and comedian Bill Cosby and his comic relief would serve a valuable purpose cheering me up at times. As I got to know many of my fellow patients on the hospital's psychiatric ward, I learned that my major depression issues were somewhat minor when compared to the more serious problems other individuals were confronted with.

As the hours and days passed during my hospital stay, I had decided to keep a journal to help release my accumulated anxiety and just to formulate my thoughts from my head and put them onto paper. I share some of the actual journal entries here:

Sunday, January 19

Today was my 7th day in the hospital and I feel somewhat confused. I stayed in bed much too long today and had a pretty intense headache all day. Andrea was in for a visit, it went very well. I thank God I have such a sweet, supportive wife; I love her dearly. I know that one of these days my feelings of hopelessness will go completely away. I know that I am a good person and a lot of my thoughts are not all that radical, I must stop analyzing all that I do. I must work on my concentration and begin to think about decisions that are facing me when I get out. I had fun playing spades today with Jerry, Vincent and Lori (nurse). My goals for this week are to open up and be more talkative (assertive), think positive and make progress in feeling better. I also want to be disciplined in getting up early for breakfast and in getting exercise when possible. I am going to close my day with reading and prayer and call it a day.

Tuesday, January 21

Today I got up at 7:30 after meeting with Dr. Hoffer. We discussed my lack of progress and the strategies we would take to show improvement. We had two groups; I don't feel I'm getting much from the group therapy but I still want to participate. I need to curb my eating a bit and get more exercise. Andrea called tonight and got upset somewhat; I know I must get better not only for myself but for her and the baby because they need me. Lord help me to combat my negative thoughts and to start to get better. My goals for tomorrow are to get up on time and be happy, cheerful and positive. With that I'll call it a day.

Wednesday, January 22

Today I got up at 7:00 and went to breakfast. I attended community group at 7:30 and went back to bed until lunch. I had a frustrating day because I am looking hard for improvement in my attitude and behavior. I want to be happy and cheerful but I try to pull myself up and end up going back down. I wish I had my entire mind back again; it feels like there's something missing. I am

*praying that my mind will return to normal and I can
have the discipline to go on with living. My situation
is so confusing that I don't know where to start to make
progress - I MUST GET BETTER. I would like to be
more disciplined tomorrow and not be so analytical. I have
a lot of support from friends and family and am hopeful
that in time this awful feeling will pass. God help me to
work at getting better. "I will put all my worries in God's
hands."*

Saturday, January 25

*A slow starter but overall a good day. I woke up early in
the am but lay in bed until 10:45. I showered and shaved
and then went to lunch. Andrea, Mom and Dad arrived
at one o'clock for visiting hours. We had a very pleasant
visit and I made some decisions. I decided to abandon
my Amway pursuit and God, I ask you to help keep my
mind off of these anxiety producing thoughts and off of the
business as a whole. Help me to change my thinking, in
part, back to the Al before Amway. I need to consciously
block out the programming I received in order to recognize
my true potential. Areas I need to work on include self-
esteem, concentration and decision making. Lord help me
get well soon! Until tomorrow...*

Sunday, January 26

I got out of bed at 11:00 and attended a group after eating lunch, Andrea, Mom, Dad and I met with Dr. Hoffer. The meeting went well and I feel I am progressing and I pray that God will help me beat this thing. Andrea, Mom and Dad stayed visiting with me until 4:00. After they left, I went out for a jog. I came back in and did some sit ups then went to dinner. After dinner I decorated the group lounge for the football game and took a shower. I watched the Super bowl where the Redskins beat the Bills 37-24. Overall, I feel my day went fairly well. I hope to continue my progress so that I can go home by the end of the week. Reflecting back on this weekend, I thank God for such wonderful parents that are so supportive of me. My goal for tomorrow is to get out of bed when the alarm goes off and to maintain a positive attitude all day long. Lord help me block out the negative thoughts and help me put AMWAY behind me. And help me be disciplined yet not be too hard on myself so that new opportunities –doors– will open. Thank you God for making me realize that I can't make it through life alone, I need you!

Seeing firsthand that I was not so bad off when compared to some of the other patients on the ward helped me realize that I could eventually make it out of this place of refuge for the weary souls. One young lady, a local college student, had attempted suicide by cutting her wrists, and I later learned that she had done this many times before. How someone so young could have the same depths of depression that I had was beyond my scope of understanding. Another young woman had experienced high levels of mania from her diagnosed condition of bipolar disorder. The visions of grandeur coupled with her many dramatic productions were sometimes comical to the rest of us in this otherwise boring and depressive psychiatric institution. Another of my fellow ward mates, a young man who had experienced unresponsive depression for many years, was to undergo shock treatments as a last attempt to find some relief from the unending mental torment he had faced for quite some time. Another individual I had come in contact with while in the psychiatric institution was fighting the darkness also, but his emotional outlet had been a constant desire for food. Vincent was a very large, black man who worked for the Department of Corrections in upstate Virginia and was making progress on his eating disorder and accompanying depression. He was an extremely polite person and a pleasure to be around. We often played cards together to pass the time as we searched for the key to wellness.

With all my heart, I hoped and prayed that my condition would eventually respond to traditional medication. Extremely scared that the darkness would never end, I made the commitment to persevere until that day of relief would come. I waited patiently for the rejuvenating light that would eventually penetrate the stubborn depression and brighten my future days. While making my recovery in the psychiatric hospital, my dear wife Andrea visited often and my wonderful parents ensured me that, "Everything would be okay!" Constant family support and Pastor Bamberger's faith-filled visits helped to eventually lift my spirit from the depths of total darkness.

Several of the doctors on staff had taken keen interest in my still somewhat unresponsive condition. After pressuring Dr. Hoffer to make some aggressive changes in my medicine, I began to obtain some limited relief from the overwhelming depression that had strangled my life for some time. Upon my hospitalization departure, this new combination of medicines, Lithobid, Pamelor and Xanax, seemed to be helping somewhat, but I was still only marginally stable. The cost of inpatient psychiatric care was ridiculously expensive. After only fourteen days of hospitalization I left the psychiatric institution. I checked myself out not because I was better, but because I learned that my charges were exceeding $1,000 a day and my health insurance was nearly exhausted. It's amazing that many health insurance companies today still discriminate against illnesses of the most important body part – the brain, or one's mind. My $20,000 lifetime limit on mental healthcare had all but run out during my two-week hospital stay. I was discharged from the hospital on January 27, 1992, on a "wing and a prayer," a very large prayer as a matter of fact!

Chapter Seven
A Ray of Light

Shortly after being discharged from my one and only psychiatric hospitalization, the first door of opportunity was opened for me. I received a call from my airline's human resources department and was asked if I would be interested in a parts clerk position in the maintenance division. After a brief discussion with my wife, I thought this to be an important first step in getting back to gainful employment, and within a few hours I notified the personnel representative that I was indeed very interested in this position. Based on my past employment record with the airline, this job was offered to me over the phone and I accepted graciously. I would start within the week and was told to contact the Manager of Stores at the company's hangar at the Richmond International Airport. Andy Wright was my new manager's name, and upon contacting him he told me when and where to report for duty.

The full-time position as a parts clerk in the airline's maintenance department was a significant step backwards from my previous job as a pilot for the flight operations division; however, at the time I considered this new employment opportunity to be a true Godsend. Although it did not offer the monetary compensation I was accustomed to in the past, I enthusiastically accepted the position because it would be initially based in Richmond and more importantly, my family health benefits were due to expire soon due to the length of my medical leave of absence. My pilot contract at that time discontinued all compensation and health benefits after being off work for more than 180 days. This window of opportunity had opened just in time allowing all my company benefits to continue uninterrupted. I could now have some piece of mind having my wife and soon to be additional family member covered under a very comprehensive and inexpensive insurance plan.

In February of 1992, a few days prior to being a leap baby, my first son, Brydon Jeffrey, arrived into our lives. I was still struggling with the darkness, but the experience of his birth left me totally awestruck. In the delivery room, I think the doctor and nurses were more concerned with me rather than Brydon and his mother. I was extremely emotional and the tears of joy drowned the months of emptiness and sadness the darkness brought about. After Andrea and I gratefully rejoiced in the arrival of our new son, the pediatrician came in with some unfortunate and rather upsetting news. We were told that Brydon's x-rays showed some fluid on the lungs that they were concerned about. As a precaution to prevent the onset of pneumonia, she informed us he would have to stay in the Neonatal Intensive Care Unit (NICU) for awhile to ensure his chest cleared of the amniotic fluid that was most likely ingested during his somewhat stressful delivery.

Andrea and I were pretty upset about what we had heard, but we understood that our new baby was in the best of care and that he would surely be alright. Our little boy spent the first ten days of his life in the NICU hooked up to wires, monitors and oxygen tubes. When I took Andrea home from the hospital without our little bundle of joy, we were both pretty emotional, first my institutionalization just a month prior to Brydon's arrival and now his complications requiring further hospitalization. We spent a great deal of time in the NICU the next several days. The doctors and nurses kept us informed of our infant son's progress and we anxiously waited the day we could take him home to his new nursery. I had forced myself to prepare our home for the baby's arrival by spending a considerable amount of time painting and bordering our little one's bedroom. I must say it looked quite nice when it was finally finished.

While accompanying Brydon in the NICU, we spent time with a couple from our church. Chip and Elaine Morton had twins a few weeks prior, and their girls were born prematurely with some rather serious complications. Ten days later, we were able to take our son home, and Brydon gave me a whole new meaning for wanting to live. Not being so fortunate, Elaine and Chip's twins would have to stay in the NICU for several months. A lot of love, many prayers and by the grace of God, eventually the girls went home healthy and sound.

Shortly after the birth of our son, my job transferred to the northern Virginia area at the Washington Dulles International Airport. This relocation was no surprise as I was told that my position would be moving northward as the company closed its Richmond maintenance facility. The commute to my new work location, between our home in Glen Allen and Chantilly, Virginia, just west of the Washington, D.C. area, was two and one half hours each way. Fortunately, my good friend Pat and his wife Kristina, having made the move to Northern Virginia earlier that year, offered a spare bedroom in their Leesburg, Virginia, townhouse for me to stay a few nights a week. Their kindness and generosity during some extremely difficult emotional and financial times was greatly appreciated.

I was working four ten hour days and was able to avoid the long drive back to the Richmond area several days a week by sleeping in their home. I began to feel somewhat better, but the unrelenting depression was still quite paralyzing. I found myself again worrying as before about my present struggles and the unknown difficulties that lay ahead. There were days when I literally had to pull myself out of bed and muster up enough energy to simply make it to the shower. Once I got going, the day did get a little easier, but the lingering darkness hampered nearly all of my activities, smothering most pleasurable sensations and any lurking feelings of happiness. After welcoming a new son into our world, what should have been the best of times in my life were perhaps some of the worst to handle from my on-going struggles with the darkness.

After driving to northern Virginia several times a week, it was obvious that the lengthy commute to work could not go on for an extended period of time. However, I felt it was important to continue working for the airline from which I was on medical leave as a flight officer. In order to maintain my benefits package and most importantly my healthcare coverage for myself and my family, moving closer to the Dulles airport would allow more time for us to spend together as a newly expanded family. My wife agreed that us living up in the northern Virginia area would be for the best and she was able to request a transfer to her company's satellite office in McLean, Virginia. We scheduled a trip to the D.C. area office of Andrea's Richmond-based company to meet some of her prospective co-workers, and she was offered the opportunity to make the needed transfer.

We immediately placed our small white rancher on the real estate market and began planning for a northern migration. Within days of listing our Glen Allen home, we received and accepted an offer from a local county police officer and the plans for our journey North took root. While in the Dulles area during my work trips, I was able to locate a comfortable two bedroom apartment just north of the airport in Sterling, Virginia, that was recently remodeled and reasonably priced, fitting into our reduced budget. The possibility of owning a home in the rapidly escalating northern Virginia housing market was simply out of our reach at the time. So after having Andrea see and approve of the new place, we signed a six month lease on a fourth story, two bedroom unit in the Huntingdon Ridge apartment complex.

The move to Sterling went fairly well as friends and family helped us load up all our worldly belongings into a large U-Haul™ truck. Connected to the back of the truck was a tow dolly, hauling my pizza-smelling, gray Cavalier. Andrea and Brydon followed close behind the familiar orange and white moving truck in our Chevy Blazer full of final household belongings. Remarkably, Andrea, her parents, my parents, some friends and I all survived the physically grueling process of moving our furniture, beds, clothes, dishes, etc., up to the fourth floor apartment (without an elevator) into our new home.

After settling in to our northern Virginia residence, I now had about a fifteen-minute drive to work, and my wife had only seven or eight miles to drive to her office in McLean each day. Unfortunately, her eastbound commute toward the Washington, D.C. metropolitan area, took her just over an hour each way when the traffic was normal and took much longer if there were travel issues or increased traffic congestion. Having moved closer to the central Pennsylvania area, we were now only a little over two hours away from our family and friends. Locating a competent caregiver for our young son was a remarkable blessing. Patricia Kreider lived less than a mile away from our apartment and we were able to locate her through a personal ad in the local community newspaper. Finding such a committed and caring person to watch our four-month-old boy was another true Godsend during some additional upheaval in our lives. Patricia's genuine concern and outstanding care for Brydon during his early development will never be forgotten.

I would like to go off on a short tangent while the subject of health insurance is fresh in my mind and pertinent to the situations described in the previous paragraphs and in Chapter 6. I was extremely grateful to my employer for offering me the opportunity to transfer to another position within the corporation. By facilitating this move between departments, I was able to maintain all my benefits including health insurance that was extended to all employees and family members at little or no cost.[7] The airline's employee benefit package offered outstanding medical coverage that was among the best in any industry at that time. I was extremely fortunate and very appreciative to maintain such attractive healthcare benefits and perks for my entire family. Nevertheless, one very large shortcoming of an otherwise wonderful medical coverage package had a powerful and detrimental impact on my life, and I thought it appropriate to explain my feelings and frustrations regarding this important deficiency here and now.

The attractive health insurance coverage provided to my family at little cost by the company had some major flaws when it came to providing adequate mental health benefits. Co-payment for outpatient treatment and therapy was set at fifty percent, meaning half of all costs were paid by the employee. Additionally, medication costs were not covered by a legitimate co-pay. The cost of receiving quality psychiatric care was and remains immensely expensive; furthermore, many of the newer, more effective medications were quite exorbitant in price as well. The blanket coverage limit of twenty thousand dollars, lifetime mental health benefit that was placed on my insurance benefits was the most significant factor adversely impacting my psychological wellness. The few months of outpatient treatment coupled with my two-week stay in a psychiatric hospital completely exhausted my "lifetime" benefit. Certainly anyone diagnosed with a serious disease or disorder

---

[7] The days of 100% employer paid health insurance have certainly come to an end in a new era of skyrocketing medical costs and often inadequate medical billing and processing systems.

of the mind would require extended care and on-going treatment for conditions in which often no cure exists.

While I remained employed at my current airline company, all of our "traditional" medical costs would be fully covered with minimal expense and little or no co-payment responsibilities placed upon us. However, the expenses associated with the treatment and maintenance of my inherited illness of the mind classified as a mental health cost would be borne solely from personal financial sources, mainly our saving account. I have included a copy of an insurance claim form for Outpatient Therapy with the explanation that "Maximum Benefit For This Service Has Been Paid." (shown below)

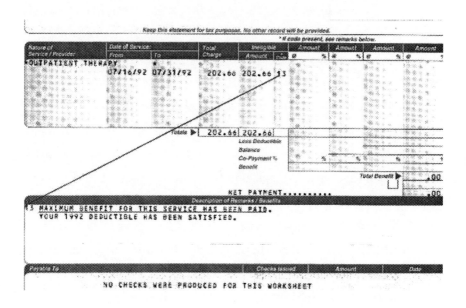

What concerns me the most about these mental health limitations and financial caps is the perception that a mental health issue may be less of a genuine illness than many other common complications such as, heart disease, diabetes, cancer, etc. If I had been born with the genetic makeup to contract one of these physical illnesses, my insurance limits would have been one million dollars. Without a doubt, the brain is the most important organ in every human being's body. Thus, a twenty-thousand dollar "lifetime" limit on healthcare for treatment of one's mind is simply ludicrous. I feel strongly that the time is now for all concerned individuals to influence our elected officials in Washington, D.C., to pass legislation guaranteeing parity among healthcare issues. Politicians must pass laws allowing equal access to quality psychiatric care to the millions of Americans who have been unfairly discriminated against when forced to provide this needed, expensive healthcare through "out of pocket" funds. Legislation for fair healthcare benefits to individuals who have been afflicted is long overdue.

Shortly after moving to northern Virginia, I began to see a new psychiatrist named Dr. Donald Grayson. Even though my mental health benefits had been exhausted, I had to continue my pursuit of relief from the continuing darkness. By employing aggressive treatment strategies, under Dr. Grayson's skillful care I made significant progress after some medication changes were enacted. He began my recovery process by sending me to a neurological specialist for a complete neurological examination.[8] The results of that evaluation were mostly a confirmation that my neurological health was fairly normal and without suspect. However, the neurologist noticed a slight nervousness and a twitching sensation in my muscle activity. His report to Dr. Grayson emphasized this one abnormality and helped us arrive at a medication mix that really turned life around for me.

Tegretol, an anti-seizure medication usually used to treat epilepsy, was introduced and the Lithobid and Pamelor mix that I had been on since leaving the hospital in Richmond was discontinued. I had experienced only limited relief from the Pamelor and the side effect

---

[8] Fortunately and ironically this examination was fully covered under my insurance benefits because it was considered a medical procedure, not "mental" healthcare.

profile of headaches and an extremely dry mouth had been discomforting for quite some time. Klonopin, a longer lasting anti-anxiety medication, was added in place of Xanax in order to help me sleep better through the night. This combination of Tegretol and Klonopin provided almost immediate improvement to my stable, yet mediocre condition.

By the fall of 1992, the gloominess and shadows that had darkened my life for over a year had finally begun to lift. Feelings of pleasure and happiness started to work their way back into my everyday life. My mind was slowly returning to a "normal" state and my old self seemed to be coming alive again. One very pleasant memory and experience that has stuck in my mind to this day began with the purchase of two tickets to the famous Broadway musical "CATS" that was playing in Washington, D.C., at the National Theater. I secretly bought the tickets and planned to surprise my wife with a night on the town in celebration of her birthday. Having dropped Brydon at the sitter's after an early dinner, we headed east to the Falls Church Metro station and caught the subway to downtown Washington.

It was still a mystery to my wife as to where I was taking her that evening. As we walked from the downtown D.C. Metro station and made a right turn and headed up 10th Street, NW, Andrea was still in the dark as to where we were going. Getting closer and closer to the theater entrance, the marquee became visible and it was an awesome sight to see the sparkle in my wife's eyes when she realized that we were going to see this delightful musical we had often talked about and dreamed of seeing. Arriving at the theater shortly before show time, the excitement I felt was almost surreal for it had been sometime since I had felt such pleasant emotions.

The orchestra's amazing rendition of Andrew Lloyd Webber's music and the cast's wonderful performance were truly magnificent. The entire show was an amazing spectacle and the quality of the night's entertainment was outstanding. Towards the end of the production as the cat, Grizabella, remembered her vibrant younger years and sang the feature song "Memory," my heart filled with warmth as the seeds were planted that would allow me to begin dreaming again, seeds that I felt would perhaps grow and enable me to experience a new beginning myself. That song still maintains a very special place in my heart and mind, because it signifies a point in my life when the rays of sun began to shine brilliantly through the darkness truly lighting my soul at last. The final words of that show-stopping song, "...*a new day has begun,*"[9] embellished my every emotion as tears of joy crept slowly down both sides of my face.

When the performance of "CATS" was finished, leaving the theater and returning to the Metro station was very exhilarating and somewhat sentimental. As we approached the top of the Archives/Navy Memorial Metro entrance, many homeless people were huddled closely to watch the theater crowd leave our nation's capital for all points hoping to collect some monetary hand-outs. During my deep depression, I often pictured myself being destitute and one day living on the street, but I was feeling uplifted as we descended the steps to the subway platform knowing that I had not ended up in such a dire situation. While feeling good about myself, I felt deep concern for the homeless individuals we had seen only moments earlier. I seriously contemplated how many of them might be lifted from their plights with the support and quality physical and mental health care that I had at my disposal. I prayed for God to bless them and help them as He had done for me.

As I write of this amazingly uplifting and climactic turning point in my mental health recovery process and reflect back on the events of that evening,

---

[9]   The last line from the CATS Broadway musical song "Memory" written by Andrew Lloyd Webber and performed by Natalie Toro that night at the National Theater

something mysteriously popped into my thoughts. Many years ago, one of this country's greatest leaders, who himself experienced tremendous inner darkness and mental anguish, coincidentally was assassinated at the same location that housed this riveting dramatic performance, which provided the catalyst for my rejuvenated and ascending spirit. Abraham Lincoln, the 16th President of the United States, had reportedly suffered many bouts of severe depression over his lifetime.

On the night of Good Friday, April 14, 1865, from his executive box just to the right of the balcony where my wife and I had sat 127 years later, President Lincoln was mortally wounded from the gun shot fired by actor John Wilkes Booth in what was then known only as Ford's Theater. Lincoln never regained consciousness and was pronounced dead early the next morning at the Petersen Boarding House directly across 10th Street, NW.

Shortly after this revitalizing experience, life began to become brighter each day. It was the beginning of my escape from the darkness and my return to a bright new world. I started envisioning many new horizons that only months before would have barely peeked my interest. One of these newfound excitements was a fascination with photography and Artistic Expressions (AE), my self-propelled photographic venture, was soon born. The possibility of becoming a freelance photographer – capturing beautiful landscapes, brilliant sunsets and sunrises as well as captivating wildlife seemed quite appealing to me. I enjoyed snapping just the right shot and then finding a Scripture verse that complimented or characterized the photo to be matted and framed together. I have displayed some of my creations at craft shows and consignment shops and was even able to sell a half dozen or so photos without ever getting too serious about it. I also gave some of my works to friends as gifts for birthdays and Christmas presents. My love for photography is still alive today, and my works are proudly displayed in my home and my parents' home. I have always dreamed of turning my photo ventures into more than just a hobby. Maybe in time, I will be able to pursue my love for this art form supporting myself as a professional photographer.

Around this time, a very significant individual entered my life that would later be identified as another one of my "guardian angels." Steven Douglas was an aircraft mechanic who worked with me on a daily basis in my new parts clerk position within the airline's maintenance department. I had met Steve a year or so earlier while I was still flying as a pilot, and he was "wrenching" (as he called it) the aircraft flying out of the Richmond domicile. After working with Steve day in and day out, a very special friendship developed that still lasts to this day. He was and remains a very conscientious and hard-working employee. Steve would always find something to do, even if it meant picking up a broom to sweep around the maintenance office, aircraft ramp or parts area. His love for life itself and his deep rooted faith were powerfully evident in all that he did. His work ethic, positive attitude and "get it done" mentality were quite an invigorating change from most of the individuals with whom we worked. I always enjoyed our lively discussions which Steve liked to call "Raps" and found them very uplifting.

Our relationship blossomed into a true friendship founded in our mutual respect and love for the Lord. Steve's inner light was so bright in my life that the days of darkness gradually began to fade from my recent memory. Steve invited Andrea, who often referred to him as "the Squirrel Man,"[10] Brydon and I out to his mountain home near Front Royal, Virginia, to meet his wife Kathy and their three boys. We had a great time eating a wonderful dinner and getting to know my good friend's family. It was at Steve and Kathy's home out on the mountain that he made a comment about the license plate on my Chevy Blazer. The last three digits of the plate were "666," and unbeknown to me,

---

[10] At that time in his life, Steve was pretty heavy and had a thick beard, closely resembling the legendary mountain character "Grizzly Adams."

he informed me that this number was biblically symbolic for "the sign" of the devil.[11] I considered myself fairly versed in the Scriptures, but I was naïve to this reference that would reveal a meaningful significance later in my life (Chapter 8 - The Awakening).

In addition to our God-centered friendship, Steve and I loved to hunt and we became the best of hunting buddies. The fall of 1992 was the most exciting and productive year of hunting I have ever experienced thanks to my great friend. Deer hunting was our passion, and I was fortunate to bag three whitetail bucks that fall season during hunting trips in Virginia and in Pennsylvania. My success in harvesting the Virginia deer was directly attributed to Steve's prowess and expertise in the woods. With his knowledge and patience, I took up archery hunting for the first time and after much practice felt confident enough to take the bow out to the woods in search of a trophy whitetail buck.

Through another work associate, we had been provided access to some prime hunting land nearby. Steve and I were hunting as often as we could together or by ourselves when our schedules conflicted. We were able to locate an old, large, branching oak tree that was well-positioned in a small strip of woods surrounded by soybean fields on three sides. This historic oak provided the ideal location for our deer hunts, and we made sure that someone was in this tree morning and evening as much as possible during the short two-week archery season. I had spent a fair amount of time in that tree during the season and saw many deer and a few good bucks. Up to now, I was not able to have a mature antlered deer come within bow range while spending relaxing time in our special spot, the old oak tree.

One morning before work, I was comfortably nestled in the tree when a seven-point buck came out of the woods behind the old oak

[11] "Whoever is intelligent can figure out the meaning of the number of the beast... Its number is 666." Revelation13:18

75

and proceeded to walk along the edge of the field right toward me. As I positioned myself properly to take a possible shot, my heart began to race uncontrollably. The nice seven pointer positioned himself about fifteen yards from my vantage point in the old scraggly oak. As I released the arrow from my Fred Bear starter bow, I carefully followed the arrow's path and was confident of a good hit as I saw the bright green and white arrow fletches flash in the morning sun as the whitetail barreled off. The excitement of the hunt was overwhelming as I had shot the first buck of my lifetime using a primitive weapon, the bow and arrow. If you are not a hunter or dislike those who hunt, please bear with me! The remaining sections detailing my hunting adventures serve as monumental experiences in my uphill struggle against the once suffocating darkness.

After a few minutes, I got down from the old oak and briefly searched for the deer's trail. Running short on time, since I had to be at work by 9:00 AM, I abandoned my tracking pursuit and would have to come back later that day to resume the search. Once at work, I immediately told Steve of the morning's events and he agreed to go look for the deer after he finished his shift. I was able to clear it with my boss to leave early that afternoon to accompany Steve on our attempt to search for and hopefully recover the buck I shot earlier that day. On the drive to our hunting spot, he warned me that picking up the trail this late in the day could prove to be an impossible task. I remained confident even though Steve's years of experience attempted to persuade me into the realization that finding this buck would be almost impossible. When we arrived at the tree where I had taken the shot many hours earlier, the initial trail I had followed now lead to a dead end. As we walked out into the adjoining soybean field, Steve noticed a lone buzzard fly from a barren tree several hundred yards away. His intuition led him to believe that the deer was laying dead in this field somewhere.

We quickly walked to the vicinity of the barren tree. By now the sun was getting lower in the western sky and all traces of daylight would soon fade away. Using his powerful binoculars, Steve scanned the field carefully looking for any unusual clumps of brown that might indicate a fallen deer. After several minutes of scanning the field around us, he paused saying he saw something off in the distance that might be the buck. As we walked in the direction, ironically back toward the big old oak, I could not believe my eyes as we approached the seven pointer laying in the field only about a hundred yards from our treasured tree. Imagine the sun beginning to set on a soybean field in northern Virginia as two grown men are dancing, embracing and crying out praises to God for their amazing find. Jubilation was the feeling of the moment and after the joyous celebration mellowed somewhat, we both got down on our knees to give thanks to the One that truly makes all things possible. It was then and there I realized I had a true God brother for life. The warmth and completeness felt in that soybean field that fall evening has stayed with me and will remain a part of my soul forever.

Because of his work schedule, Steve was unable to hunt the first day of the Virginia firearms season. He had been scouting deer in an area near his home in the George Washington National Forest for some time and agreed to put me on a spot he thought might produce another fine whitetail. While at work a few nights before opening day of rifle season, we sat down in the break area under the midfield concourse, and Steve drew me a map detailing exactly where he had seen some promising deer scrapes and buck rub signs. It involved parking at a certain spot, wading across a trout stream and locating a ravine several hundred yards away. He drew the map with meticulous accuracy as he labeled points along the way. I had only been to this location once before on a springtime trout-fishing expedition, and finding this hunting spot in the cover of darkness would be exceedingly challenging.

In the interest of making a long story short, I followed the map precisely and when dawn broke that first morning, the answer to a deer-hunter's prayer would be revealed. A high-antlered, six point buck stepped into my sight and the crack of my rifle in the crisp morning air caused the buck to fall immediately. Later that week Steve proceeded to the sight where he wanted me to be that morning. There he found my lone bullet casing lying within ten yards of where his map had intended me to be. Both of us were somewhat astonished with the successful outcome of yet another hunting adventure that we carefully planned and flawlessly executed. However, we were quick to realize that Someone upstairs had been watching over us and blessing us to make our earthly plans work to perfection.

> *"Steve, the amazing accuracy that you provided in mapping out my return to wholeness was astounding. Our friendship, teamwork and great faith allowed me to see the joys of life once again. You helped bring me back from the darkness and helped restore fullness to my once lost soul. For that I am eternally grateful, my friend and brother in the Lord. Thanks Buddy!"*

I was fortunate enough to harvest three nice bucks (one in Pennsylvania as well) during that memorable hunting season. The same year that had begun in a psychiatric institution, later welcoming my beloved son into the world, and finally learning to live again and regaining my zest for life primarily from the kindness and love of my faithful "God brother" Steve.

With the remarkable progress I had made during the later part of 1992, I began to dream of returning to the piloting profession that

I had once loved and missed so much. After my sleep patterns had completely returned to normal and the depression had totally lifted, I felt I was ready to attempt the final phase in my recovery process. Late in December 1992 with my doctor's concurrence, we decided that the depths of darkness were pushed completely into remission, and I would slowly phase off the medication in an attempt to discontinue all medication by the first of the year. Beginning the New Year of 1993, the plan to become free of the once-needed stabilizing agent and anti-anxiety drug was the resolution. On January 1st, I stopped taking all medications with the hope of returning to the skies after a mandatory three-month waiting period. This 90-day waiting period was mandated by the Federal Aviation Administration, and I was confident that the time would sail by uneventfully. My mood was very positive and the once desperate darkness was now a very distant memory. It appeared that my life and my career were finally back on track.

CHAPTER EIGHT
THE AWAKENING

Shortly after the beginning of the New Year, I had just turned twenty-eight years old and was anxiously anticipating the completion of the ninety-day medication free waiting period required by the Federal Aviation Administration (FAA) Aeromedical Branch. Hopefully, in a few months I would once again be able to return to the cockpit and resume the piloting career that I had so passionately missed. It had been over eighteen months since I had last flown an airplane and my desire to return to the flight deck was monumental. As the first several weeks of 1993 passed, my once devastating depression showed no sign of return, but I slowly began to experience some difficulty sleeping. The keen desire to remain off medication and an unrelenting drive to return to my beloved flying profession gave me the strength and stamina to maintain my mental health while experiencing the onset of additional sleep deprivation.

Dr. Grayson wrote a detailed summary of my recovery for the FAA, outlining a complete rehabilitation from a major depressive episode and the total discontinuation of medication that had been prescribed to treat my condition. In his final analysis and psychiatric evaluation, he made the recommendations that would pave the way for me to return to the aviation career I had worked so hard to develop prior to the time when the engulfing darkness invaded my life. The FAA scheduled me to meet with their own staff psychiatrist in the later part of April, and if their psychiatric consultant concurred with my personal physician's findings, I would once again be authorized to occupy a pilot's seat aboard a commercial airliner. April could not come soon enough! The deep motivation to resume my piloting career coupled with the desire to have my life return back to normal, both professionally and financially, was a powerful inspirational force during these often anxious and once again sleepless times.

My wife and I along with our son Brydon, who had turned one year old in February, began to make preliminary plans regarding a desired move back to the central Pennsylvania area. Once I had returned to my piloting position, the plan was for me to commute to my work domicile at the Washington Dulles International Airport (IAD) from the Harrisburg International Airport (HIA) located in Middletown, Pennsylvania. We began searching for building lots within thirty minutes of HIA and eventually located a beautiful parcel of land along Ridge Road just southeast of the borough of Elizabethtown.

The lot on which we were planning to build was located on an elevated ridgeline offering a tremendous view of the neighboring farmland and the picturesque countryside. After making a down payment on the building lot, my father helped us draw up some general plans for our modest little dream home. A very close friend of our family, agreed to draft detailed renderings of our proposed 2,200 square foot home to be constructed of wood and stone. Joy and excitement had returned to our daily lives, and I was elated to see that the hopes and dreams we had once imagined appeared to be coming to fruition.

Unfortunately, by the first week in March, my sleeping routine had deteriorated to only a few hours a night. I knew full-well that my doctor should have been told of my worsening sleep deprivation, but all of our plans were contingent upon my return to employment as a pilot. I would continue to persevere while hoping and praying that my sleep would eventually return to normal. Issues at work were now quite complicated and the increased stress and worries from this situation were also loading down my ability to remain mentally well.

The airline that had employed me for nearly four years had been experiencing some challenging operational times and financial troubles. Recently, a major airline had purchased our much smaller company and now controlled the fate of this once prosperous regional subsidiary. Shrewd business decisions dictated the somewhat undesirable outcome of a once mighty and highly respected midwestern air carrier. Our company would be dissolved and the ensuing liquidation would involve the sale of assets to two new corporate entities and also to a third established regional airline. The Dulles International operation, the division where I was employed, would be acquired by a small east coast carrier based in Sterling, Virginia.

Through agreements negotiated by the national pilots' union, I was able to exercise bidding rights through the seniority integration process and decided to transfer to the east coast acquiring company, still with principal operations at Washington's Dulles Airport. It appeared I would certainly be able to hold a relatively senior pilot position at the new company; however, under a new pay structure our salaries, previously some of the most attractive in the industry, would be reduced by nearly forty percent. Most of the ground personnel were also offered employment at the acquiring company for significantly less compensation and reduced healthcare coverage as well.

For obvious financial reasons, I decided not to transfer to the new company in my current position in the maintenance department. Therefore, at the end of March I would be laid off, eligible for unemployment benefits and possibly qualify for job retraining if needed. The sought-after plan would have me exercising my seniority rights and returning to the cockpit as a Captain for the acquiring regional airline after the FAA's psychiatrist had cleared me to fly. The stress from all this employment uncertainty, the looming reduction in salary and my deteriorating ability to sleep, once again began to place an extremely heavy burden on my body and mind. My mood remained fairly upbeat, while I was numbly aware of the frightening reality of my fragile mental health deteriorating with each passing day.

Our family of three planned a trip back to Pennsylvania to visit friends and relatives and to spend a weekend in the area that soon we would call home once again. During the visit, a powerful Nor'easter later deemed the "Blizzard of the Century"[12] hit Lancaster County and surrounding areas with a paralyzing blow. Andrea, Brydon and I ended up getting stranded at my in-laws for a few extra days as the Governor of Pennsylvania declared a state of emergency and all travel on the roadways of the Commonwealth were restricted to snow removal equipment and emergency vehicles only. The time we spent snowed in at Andrea's parents was somewhat relaxing, and I was able to venture out into the vast blanket of white snow and icicles to take some very beautiful pictures of the pristine countryside. We stayed in Pennsylvania until the state of emergency was lifted and the roads were cleared and passable. We then loaded up our Chevy Blazer and headed out into the beautiful snow-covered farmlands on our southern track back to northern Virginia.

I was now in my last few weeks of work since the transfer of assets to the acquiring company was scheduled to take place on April 1st. The

---

[12]   On March 13, 1993, a large storm dumped between two and three feet of snow and caused high winds, creating monstrous drifts in communities from Washington, D.C. to Boston, MA.

combined stress of work coming to an end coupled with the lack of sleep had now become quite overwhelming. During these very frantic and uncertain times, one morning we received a call from my mother-in-law informing us that Andrea's Father was in the hospital. He had experienced a heart attack the night before and was being prepared to undergo surgery to correct multiple blockages of the blood passages leading to and from his heart. His by-pass surgery was scheduled for later that day and both Andrea and I were very concerned for her father's health and quite upset at the thoughts of an unsuccessful resolution to his heart problems.

My father-in-law, Henry, had always been a very relaxed, gentle and hard-working man. He and I were pretty close, and we often spent many summer days on local golf courses attempting to hit that little white ball down the fairways, onto the green and eventually into the hole marked by a numbered flagstick. My in-laws seldom attended church, and I was worried that Henry might not make it through the surgery. From earlier experiences of doubting my own faith, I was deeply concerned that my friend and father-in-law would be called home before I truly knew where he stood in his personal relationship with "his Maker." I could only pray for God to take care of Henry and see him successfully through the delicate procedure he was about to undergo that day. The worry of him not pulling through this risky surgical operation and some how not making it past St. Peter at the pearly gates, played extremely heavy on my already weary soul.

By the last week in March, my condition had deteriorated considerably and I was now literally unable to sleep at all. As a result, my ability to think, reason and concentrate was becoming somewhat compromised. I was also experiencing challenging body fatigue. Under these trying conditions, my emotional well being had become quite unstable. My wavering mental state caused me to experience an array of emotions, and I even found myself crying in the shower at times for no apparent reason. While attempting to keep these emotional outbreaks from Andrea, the feelings I had been experiencing were very strange, even quite confusing during certain periods. I was terribly disappointed and saddened over the reality of my once again deteriorating health. Would I have to endure the darkness again? However, at times I felt great joy and comfort from what seemed to be a very powerful, invisible force pulling me through life.

At this point I began to realize that my vision of successfully returning to my once beloved flying profession, moving my family back home to central Pennsylvania and building our little dream house was certainly not going to materialize. It was obvious that my delicate mental health was again going to need aggressive attention and medication to control the continuing inability to rest my weary body and mind. The crystal ball which just months ago was so bright and held such great promise lay shattered before my very eyes.

Still refusing to accept the inevitable, I attempted to keep busy during my many sleepless nights by not only watching television and videos but also by undertaking various projects and reading the Bible. I accomplished a significant amount of work on my expanding photography collection, purged many old files containing outdated personal material and even decided to thoroughly update my résumé. Trying to focus and concentrate on these many nocturnal projects became increasingly difficult as the fatigue from being awake for so many hours continued to take its toll. One night while updating the supplement to my résumé which provided my official career references, I remember crossing out two individuals with whom I had not seen or corresponded in many years.

The first reference I deleted from my list was a friend and fellow pilot named John Sterner. He and I had worked and flown together early in my aviation career, and John was now the Director of Program Development for the Aircraft Owners and Pilots Association's (AOPA) Air Safety Foundation headquartered in Frederick, Maryland. He was a great co-worker and served somewhat as a mentor in my earlier years of professional aviating. I had not spoken to nor seen John in many years and thought it best to remove him from this list of references. The second individual I crossed off my reference list was Dr. H.D. Wilson, my former high school principal and now additionally the President-Elect of the National Association of Secondary School Principals located in Reston, VA. It had been nearly ten years since I had any meaningful contact with Dr. Wilson and decided his removal from the list also seemed pertinent at the time.

The previous divine guidance that I had felt leading me through life was never more apparent only a few days after eliminating the two individuals from my résumé references supplement. Both of these fine gentlemen mysteriously came back into my life almost at the same time. On March 24, 1993, while in the process of running some errands at work, I noticed John standing in the passenger waiting area by my company's departure and arrival gates. I approached him and we excitedly greeted each other. We began to talk about our present careers, catching up on lost time. After conversing for several minutes, John handed me his AOPA business card and told me not to hesitate calling him if he could help me in any way. I was rather astounded to have John ironically return into my life after consciously writing him off as simply a historical memory only a few nights earlier. In my mind, the mysterious hand of God was sending an old friend to bring hope to my somewhat broken soul, just when I needed it most.

The very next day, while also in the passenger boarding area, I was both shocked and amazed beyond belief to see Dr. Wilson waiting by our gates in the main terminal at Dulles International Airport.

I was overcome with emotion as I could not contain the feelings of unexplained happiness and joy that rushed through my entire being. Through the jubilant feelings and the flowing tears, I tried to explain all that had happened in my life since I had last seen my trustworthy high school principal. He seemed to have an intense understanding of my feelings and an almost eerie knowledge of what I was going through. Dr. Wilson explained that he himself had experienced some very trying experiences while navigating through remarkably challenging times in raising his oldest child, a daughter who had unexplainably run away from home. His words of assurance and demonstrated concern for me were extremely comforting. In fact, one of the statements he made to me, "Just Listen!" has remained a vital part of my being to this very day.

Dr. Wilson was a highly supportive administrator during my high school years and always challenged my abilities by expecting a little more out of me than he would any other student. He was sympathetic and caring when my brother died back in 1981, and I believe he tried to provide additional oversight and guidance in an attempt to push me to greater heights than I would have attained without his intervention. Now several years later, he was calming me down and comforting my anxiety with his words of reassurance. He gently and reverently spoke those memorable words, "Just Listen!" By the manner of his speech and the tone of his voice, it was obvious that he had some level of knowledge that presently was beyond my comprehension. It took some time for his prophetic words to sink in, but today I am pretty sure I fully understand what he meant.

Through careful listening and disciplined patience, God will clearly provide a path for us to follow, guiding us through life a day at a time. An amazingly clear direction will be unveiled if one truly attempts to live a righteous and virtuous existence, surrendering control to the

"Great Chief Pilot in the Sky" and Him alone. As the popular bumper stickers say, "God is my co-pilot" and "God is my pilot," only the latter will bring the peace and guidance that most human beings yearn for all their born days. This simplistic view may sound a little far-fetched, but I believe without a doubt this it what has occurred in my life and my testimony should hereby serve as powerful evidence supporting this concept.

When I left work that afternoon, I remained rather excited having seen John the day before and Dr. Wilson earlier in the day. As I drove home, the idea of seeing the two individuals I had crossed off my list of references just days before seemed surreal and dreamlike. I pondered intently the significance of both these men of important stature now returning to my life and how "Just Listening" would shape my existence in the days, weeks and years to come. Little did I know what lay in store for me after returning home that evening.

On the night of March 25, 1993, after experiencing an emotional day at work having seen my former high school principal, I would experience the most mysterious and powerful phenomenon of my lifetime which has undoubtedly changed me forever. For most of my adult life up to this point, I had been a chronic worrier, sometimes allowing worry to cripple my very being, which provided opportunities for the darkness to slip in and invade my happiness. Late that night, while my psyche was still stirred from an exhilarating yet exhausting day, I engaged in a heavy emotional outpouring to my wife resulting from the overwhelming stress and realization of our shattered dreams. As I laid out all my concerns and heartaches to her, the tears flowed profusely from my sleep-weary eyes. Two important issues remained extremely heavy on my tired soul and seemed to have my spirit tied up in unending torment.

As I searched deep inside for the strength to address these remaining worries, I asked my wife and God indirectly, "Where was my brother?" and "Would I play golf in heaven with her father?" After that emotionally draining confession of my two remaining fears, my soul felt completely empty and an amazing calm settled over me. Andrea had patiently listened, and God seemed to take away all my burdens. It is my belief that only after you give all your worries to the Lord, then and only then, will you truly know Him and His lasting peace.[13] With this remarkable calm and total peace I now felt, I was able to lie down and just prior to the midnight hour, I at last fell into a deep and sound sleep. This liberating feeling of a "freed soul" allowed my rest and dreams to be unlike anything I have ever known before nor have experienced since.

I awoke just after 4:30 AM on the morning of March 26th and was unexplainably compelled to get out of bed and head down the hallway where I quietly sat down at the dining room table. With only four and a half hours of sleep under my belt, I felt remarkably rested and the amazing tranquility that had been with me the night before was still present. After sitting quietly at the table for a few minutes in the darkness of the early morning hours, I remember slowly arching my neck backward and raising my head upward. While patiently staring at the ceiling, I felt like I was in a trance as the most astonishing experience of my life was about to unfold.

The "awakening" started with a vision of what appeared to be a long tunnel opening before my very eyes. As I began to clearly see this hollow tube-like vision extend through the ceiling into a vast space of darkness, an extremely brilliant, almost blinding light hovered around the far end of the tunnel. This extremely bright aura slowly moved toward the far

---

13   "I sought the Lord, and he heard me, and delivered me from all my fears." PSALM 34:4

opening of the elongated cylinder and eventually moved directly into my line of sight. The magnificent light then began to move down the long tunnel, picking up speed as it traveled directly toward me. Within a few seconds, the brilliant light reached the near end of the tunnel striking me squarely in the forehead. The tremendous energy from the amazing light seemingly passed through my body. After exiting, it proceeded down the hallway toward my son's bedroom. As the light traveled down the hall and made a quick right turn into Brydon's room, I heard him let out a loud shrill as the last remnants of the once radiant, meteor-like glow faded into the early morning darkness.

When the descending comet of light impacted my forehead, my nose began to bleed profusely from the force of this mighty collision. I was able to remember feeling very euphoric, almost like "an angel," and a true sense of heightened awareness was immediately present. I quickly found pen and paper and began to record what I had just experienced. I also attempted to write down the massive amounts of knowledge and inspirations being generated by what now seemed to be my amazingly supercharged brain. These writings were very prophetic in nature, as I felt like I was a conduit of the Holy Spirit immediately following this astounding event. I do not remember much following the first few hours of this phenomenon occurring, but I have a fair amount of writings, notes and sketches that took place after my mysterious encounter with "the Light." The many days and nights of sleeplessness coupled with my body's total fatigue certainly played a significant role in this unexplainable experience, known as a "psychotic episode" or psychosis in medical terms.

I do know that Andrea awoke following all the commotion and was trying to help me calm down and attempted to stop my nose from bleeding. At some point, I became very delusional and started asking her to please help me. Scared and shaking, she called my parents to get some advice on what to do, but more importantly she needed some emotional support. As I became more and more agitated, I called out to her and eventually began to yell repeatedly, "Help Me, Help Me!" At some point, Andrea placed a call to emergency personnel at 911, and an ambulance was dispatched to our fourth floor Sterling apartment.

Brydon's babysitter, Patricia, heard the early morning ambulance call on her emergency scanner and called to see if everything was alright. She agreed to come immediately and take our young son to her house so Andrea could follow the ambulance carrying me to the Loudon County Hospital in Leesburg, Virginia. By the time we arrived at the hospital, I had managed to calm down somewhat but was still pretty incoherent. After the emergency room attendants made contact with my doctor, they agreed to release me into Andrea's custody for a short ride back east on Route 7 directly to Dr. Grayson's office. I faintly remembered the ride that morning to the hospital and our re-tracking back toward Sterling and my psychiatrist's office, but everything else was quite cloudy. Dr. Grayson thought it was critical to heavily sedate me as soon as possible to get me the much-needed rest I had been deprived of for so long. He initially prescribed the heavy tranquilizer Haldol supplemented with high doses of Xanax, and also re-prescribed the Tegretol and Klonopin that had worked so well in the past. This mix of medication would put my mind into a deep sleep for quite a while, or so I thought.

My parents had arrived from Pennsylvania to care for me while I remained in this state of deep sedation. Thank God for my parents, again! My Mom and Dad were willing to come to my assistance due to the fact that my medical benefits had been exhausted as discussed in the previous chapter. At this point, a self-paid hospitalization stay would have placed an extremely large financial burden on our already struggling financial situation. I do not know how we would have made it through another trying time without the care and compassion of such loving and supportive parents. I ended up missing the last scheduled week of work prior to being laid off, and it was early April until I was alert and fully back to reality and total consciousness. My mother and father stayed with us until I was stable enough to care for myself.

Later, Andrea and my parents informed me that during my sedation, my behavior was rather interesting and even sometimes quite bizarre. Between my periods of sleep and "cat naps," I often would walk around our apartment in only my underwear and sunglasses continuously writing and sometimes talking in a strange type of language which none of them were capable of understanding.[14] Reportedly, I was highly compelled to call my previous high school guidance counselor, and they said I would had taken the phone off the hook and attempted to place several calls to Ms. Phillips (as discussed in Chapter 3). I don't know if I was able to make contact with her, but my inner spirit was certainly motivated in attempting to establish this important communication link. Needless to say, I have no recollection of any of this eccentric activity that took place for over a week. I kept a collection of the many documents and writings that I felt spiritually inspired to produce during the time period from the evening of March 26 to the first days of April. I have included some of these manuscripts on the following pages.

---

[14]   Later reminding me of the scripture verse, "All of them were filled with the Holy Spirit and began to speak in other tongues as the Spirit enabled them." ACTS 2:4

Inspirational Insights

— The system works. Listen to it and develop change. Channel all energy in the direction of good.

— Stress destroys life – we as a nation must stop it before it ruins us. The forces of nature will be in tune with us if we _change_.

— Dreams do come true; with God all things are possible.

— Walk to the beat of the "great chief pilot" in the sky.

— Evil has lost (God)!

— Mental power, _mindset_, holds the key to life. "Narrow is the gate to life, and few there are who find it." Matthew 7.14

— Create _massive_ _think tank_ to change values in American Business.

Inspirational Insights written during my "Awakening"

A Major Awakening

The light has shown and this is what was communicated: A glimpse of the future showing massive change in all institutions. "The Rising Sun "is the key to this new world order. A millennium had occurred to change the face of the earth forever. By working in tune with nature we all can have a brighter, more fulfilling future. Be "fishers of men"; not chasers of the almighty dollar. Listen, relax and walk the yellow line (taxi line) God has asked us all to follow.

The way to prosperity is to bring about peace / a lasting peace. The iron curtain has fallen, we must go a be fishers of men. No more preaching, just a new beginning, an era of peace and change. So massive but we must take it one step at a time. Have faith, the son will rise again and everyone has their part in this play which is a great story. With God's help, we can change the face of the world.

A new era of peace and prosperity has begun. We all must take place in this amazing journey to leave a legacy to our children and theirs. A future filled with hope opportunity and a long-term lasting peace is at our fingertips but we must reach out and grab it, develop it and nurture it to ensure a brighter tomorrow for everyone. America has enjoyed prosperity and we must encourage worldwide prosperity; taking the lead in being stewards of the word in this world filled with need.

Al Kent
4 - 2 - 93

Prophetic words scribbled down after my experiencing "the Light"

95

Crossed out "666" on my license plate in a symbolic gesture that "the evil one"
had lost as I had written in the Inspirational Insights

Occurrences

- Music at night from "Close Encounters of the Third Kind."

- White pidgeon on the balcony.

- Brydon's moving balloon!

- Playing the song "Somewhere" from Westside Story. Bright red finch lands on the fence rail and warbles wildly.

Memorable occurrences that happened during my heightened state

Chapter Nine
An Amazing Journey

As my greatly expanded and overactive mind slowly began its return to some type of normalcy, I continued to feel that mystical force seemingly leading me through life. Certainly, most of our plans based on my return to flying had completely vanished. I was back on medication under the care of my psychiatrist and clearly diagnosed with bipolar disorder after such an extreme episode of mania. I cancelled the appointment with the Federal Aviation Administration (FAA) psychiatrist scheduled for April and it now appeared that I would probably never be allowed to fly again.[15] With the help of my doctor and the re-introduction of medication, I steadily began to reach a reasonable level of stability. It was imperative that I get back into society as soon as possible and determine where we would go and how we were going to get there.

After securing unemployment benefits, I learned I was also eligible to receive funding for job re-training under the Job Training

---

[15] Current FAA policy imposes a lifetime ban on any individual who has a history of bipolar disorder.

Partnership Act (JTPA). The number of layoffs at my employer caused the workplace displacements to fall under the plant closing statutes enacted several years before. Under this program, I could qualify to be trained in a different field or possibly continue my pursuit of a bachelor's degree from the Embry-Riddle Aeronautical University and tuition would be fully funded by JTPA resources. Normally, the program does not authorize tuition payments in pursuit of a college degree, but because I had only ten courses left to complete my degree program, an exception would be granted. I had to provide adequate documentation showing how the completion of my degree would provide new career opportunities by increasing my employment marketability. Having successfully completed the justification paperwork, my tuition assistance request was appreciatively granted. During the same time period, my wife began to search for new employment back in the central Pennsylvania area, since we no longer had any reason to stay in the expensive, rapidly expanding northern Virginia metropolis.

The force pulling me through life was still very evident in my weekly activities. Our original plans had been severely disrupted, but one day at a time new plans were beginning to take shape. While new windows of opportunity were opening, I had many interesting experiences and events that made lasting impressions on my still somewhat heightened mental state. A lot of interesting and often mysterious occurrences had been continuing to happen, but these few significant stories are quite memorable. The first situation involves a story about a balloon, my son and the babysitter. For the most part of the day I was working at home, in our fourth floor Sterling apartment, getting caught up on personal paperwork and making revised plans for the future. While sitting at my desk just off the living room, I realized it was quite late in the afternoon, close to the time I needed to pick up Brydon at the sitter's house down the street. Just as that thought had crossed my mind, I heard a strange noise emanating from across the living room.

As I looked in the direction of our balcony, I noticed the helium filled, Kevlar balloon that we had gotten Brydon for his first birthday was slowly moving across the stucco ceiling creating a somewhat eerie scratching sound. The balloon moved from the far corner of the living room, passing me at my desk and continued down the hallway, stopping immediately in front of Brydon's bedroom door. After witnessing the balloon's mysterious movement, it was apparent that I would be late to pick up my son at his sitter's. I immediately dialed the phone and when Patricia answered, I apologized for being late and assured her that I would be right down to pick him up. She explained that it was no problem at all because Brydon had been sleeping and had just wakened shortly before the phone began to ring. Many individuals might explain this situation as being highly coincidental, but my experiences tell me differently. I believe that God sometimes arranges events in certain sequences to illustrate that we are on the right path in life and to reassure us that we are not alone in this world. This was certainly one of those times.

The second amazing experience occurred along the same lines directly involving our baby boy, once again. While playing with his toys on the living room floor, he wandered over toward the sliding glass doors leading to our fourth floor balcony. As he crawled closer to the glass, I noticed a pure white pigeon had flown in and perched itself on the balcony handrail. As Brydon approached the base of the sliding glass doors, the brilliant white bird flew down to the balcony floor. Symbolic of a descending dove, the pure white, winged-creature peacefully walked toward the glass barrier from the outside. As my son noticed the bird approaching, he extended a hand outward in an attempt to touch the curious, snow white pigeon. The reality of the situation was apparent when his hand came to an abrupt stop after contacting the smooth glass surface. He held his hand there and the pigeon began to peck at the outside of the glass in an attempt to make physical contact with my son.

This awe inspiring interaction between a young child and a gentle feathered friend continued for some time. After a minute or two, the white pigeon backed slowly away from the glass door and flew calmly away into the daylight sky. I stared in amazement at this mysterious encounter between my son and this docile creature of God. I had experienced many other mysterious happenings during this period; however, these two events were by far the most memorable.

After searching for employment back in central Pennsylvania, Andrea was able to locate a position and eventually accepted a job with a construction company in the Harrisburg area. Our move northward from Virginia began to take shape, and in May 1993 we arrived at our new apartment home in Mount Joy, PA. My wife was working full-time for the Harrisburg builder as an administrative assistant and was able to provide health insurance and other benefits to our family. I worked part-time as a delivery driver and clerk at a friend's produce business in Lancaster and was also aggressively pursuing my bachelor's degree through the independent study program of the Embry-Riddle Aeronautical University.

Upon moving to Mount Joy, I began to see Dr. Nutter, because I was still experiencing difficulties attributed to my "manic break" episode earlier that year. In fact, at times my mental health was still very fragile as I continued to cycle between very steep highs and truly depressing lows once again. I would occasionally have some significant panic attacks and was highly emotional a great deal of the time. Although I had come a long way since my major manic episode in late March, I was still struggling to put my life back together. My studies, my job and my parenting responsibilities began to feel overwhelming. I labored to get out of bed some mornings and making it through the day became more and more of a challenge as time went on. The continuing cycles of highs and lows created tremendous stress in our lives and my wife began to grow weary of this unending roller coaster ride. My abilities to be a kind, nurturing and caring husband were slowly swallowed-up into the shadows of my continuing illness. Being totally engrossed in my own survival, my marriage to Andrea began to show serious signs of strain.

Dr. Nutter's years of experience and knowledge regarding bipolar disease were slowly helping me to recover. He also made some aggressive and needed medication changes. Keen wisdom and his familiarity with my family's psychological history led to his decision to put me on lithium,[16] the medication of choice to treat manic depression or bipolar disorder for many years. By the summer of 1993, I was taking Eskalith CR and Wellbutrin to help my again deteriorating condition and a reentry of the devastating darkness into my life. After taking the lithium and a new generation anti-depressant, the darkness began to lift and

---

[16] Lithium or lithium carbonate is a naturally occurring salt used to treat manic depression and was discovered by the Australian physician John Cade, who was quoted as saying "I believe the brain, like any other organ, can get sick and it can also heal." It was in 1949 when he published the first paper on the use of lithium in the treatment of acute mania. The U.S. Food and Drug Administration did not approve lithium for use until 1970.

I was making remarkable improvement. Thanks to the patience and caring of Dr. Nutter and this mix of prescribed medication, I was once again on a path back to wholeness.

The eventual effectiveness of the lithium had helped to eliminate the wild mood swings I had been experiencing for many months. Eventually, I was able to discontinue the Wellbutrin but continue on the daily regimen of lithium carbonate to this day. Dr. Nutter was truly a "guardian angel" having helped many individuals controlled by their illnesses. In years past, he had worked valiantly to try and save my brother, helped my father return to fullness and was now returning my life to me after over two years of a very frightening roller coaster ride and at times questionable survival. His abilities as a psychiatrist were astounding, and I am confident that the room he now occupies in the presence of the Great Physician is quite comfortable, probably elaborate and well-deserved. Rest high Dr. Nutter!

While in high school, I created an inspirational work in graphic arts class from my favorite poem, the classic "If –" by Rudyard Kipling. I super imposed Kipling's masterful work over a pictorial image of one of the National Basketball Association's (NBA) up and coming superstars, Hakeem Olajuwon. Hakeem, nicknamed "The Dream," had become one of the NBA's most dominant players and after having a few disappointing years, he led the Houston Rockets to a NBA Title during the 1993-94 season. Being a native of the west coast African Country of Nigeria, Hakeem had not touched a basketball until age fifteen. His last name, Olajuwon, translated in Nigerian to mean "being on top,"[17] was certainly fitting for this

---

[17] "Hakeem Olajuwon, His Decade in the NBA Has Been an Ever Ascending Journey," Sport Magazine. January 1995, pg. 42

remarkable player from the distant continent across the Atlantic Ocean. Hakeem wore the number thirty-four (34) and I attempted to center the number on the back of his jersey in the middle of the text to Kipling's poem.

I had all but forgotten about my creative work that still hangs in my parents' family room to this day. However, during the period of my heightened mania I experienced several months earlier, the poem's importance resurfaced and now gained significant meaning to my new life following that remarkable awakening experience. During the time when I was heavily sedated and walked aimlessly around our apartment in Sterling, Virginia, speaking strange words and writing almost continuously, I had boldly written repeatedly the following words *"If – answered!"* Upon returning to a fairly normal state of mind, I retrieved an additional copy of my creative work that I had maintained in an archive of my graphic arts projects from the early 1980's (see next page).

As a young man, I thoroughly enjoyed and even memorized the words of the poem. Now older, I read the poem carefully and intently realizing that Kipling's account of trials, tribulations and perseverance over all life's uncertainties had seemed to mirror my life experiences. Apparently, my mind had perceived a graduation into spiritual manhood that only my heavenly Father could attempt to fully explain. During the early summer of 1993, I was astounded to see that Rudyard Kipling's timeless poem provided the backdrop for the first "feature" story in the June publication of <u>Reader's Digest</u>. The highlighted story "You'll Be a Man, My Son!" appeared directly under the periodical's signature mark "World's Most Widely Read Magazine" on the cover of the June 1993 issue.

IF—

IF YOU CAN KEEP your head when all about you
　　Are losing theirs and blaming it on you;
If you can trust yourself when all men doubt you,
　　But make allowance for their doubting too;
If you can wait and not be tired by waiting,
　　Or, being lied about, don't deal in lies,
Or, being hated, don't give way to hating,
　　And yet don't look too good, nor talk too wise;

If you can dream–and not make dreams your master;
　　If you can think–and not make thoughts your aim;
If you can meet with triumph and disaster
　　And treat those two impostors just the same;
If you can bear to hear the truth you've spoken
　　Twisted by knaves to make a trap for fools,
Or watch the things you gave your life to broken,
　　And stoop and build'em up with wornout tools;

If you can make one heap of all your winnings
　　And risk it on one turn of pitch-and-toss,
And lose, and start again at your beginnings
　　And never breathe a word about your loss;
If you can force your heart and nerve and sinew
　　To serve your turn long after they are gone,
And so hold on when there is nothing in you
　　Except the Will which says to them: "Hold on";

If you can talk with crowds and keep your virtue,
　　Or walk with kings–nor lose the common touch;
If neither foes nor loving friends can hurt you;
　　If all men count with you, but none too much;
If you can fill the unforgiving minute
　　With sixty seconds' worth of distance run–
Yours is the Earth and everything that's in it,
　　And–which is more–you'll be a Man, my son!

　　　　　　　　　　　　- Rudyard Kipling

104

The article on page sixty-seven, subtitled "Behind the inspirational poem 'If –' lies the story of a father's love and a son's sacrifice", created a magnificent sense of amazement on my part. Kipling's inspiration for the creation of his classic poem and a story of how a young French soldier presented him with a remarkable gift was conveyed eloquently by author Suzanne Chazin. More significantly for me was the fact that over ten years earlier I had taken the stoic words from "If –" and inscribed them over the silhouette of young Hakeem Olajuwon's number *34*. I now correlated the significance of that number thirty-four, as my father-in-law Henry and I were both born on the same day – he in the winter of *'34,* and later that month my late brother, Jeff, would have turned *34*. Coincidence, maybe to some, but to my still spiritually attuned mind, this story in Reader's Digest held great meaning. To this day, when thinking of how these events unfolded, I am left awestruck and am reminded of the remarkable capabilities of our heavenly Father and His truly mysterious ways.

Please understand that for about six months this window of heightened awareness remained open, giving me remarkable insight and great inspiration. A few days before what would have been Jeff's 34th birthday, I was driving home from work when the radio in my Chevy Blazer suddenly became very loud. Just then, the driver of a car in the left-hand passing lane veered in front of me nearly running my vehicle off the road. As I braked and turned to avoid a collision with the encroaching car, I was drawn to the inscription on the driver's license plate that read: "SEU 1945." To my keenly conditioned mind, the interpretation from this event was that something would most likely happen at 7:45 PM (1945 military time) and I waited nervously for that hour to arrive. That evening, when the clock reached a quarter to eight and nothing happened, I was somewhat disappointed and concerned that this seemingly freak incident had meant nothing, and I began to feel as if the window of my heightened awareness was beginning to close. Possibly my feelings were simply manifestations of an overactive mind.

A few evenings later on June 29, 1993, also Jeff's 34th birthday, I lay on the sofa watching television with Brydon. My eyes were drawn to the VCR display that read 7:44 PM and in that instant, the clock display changed to 7:45 as the doorbell to our apartment simultaneously rang. My wife went to the door, opened it and began talking to someone on the porch. She walked back into the living room to retrieve her purse, took out her checkbook and returned to the front door. After a few minutes passed, she closed the door and again returned inside. I asked her who was at the front door and she replied, "Just a young boy selling books to raise money for his church youth group." Uncharacteristic of her, she purchased a book for Brydon titled My Friend Jesus and as she handed it to me I was somewhat mesmerized. Coincidence – I think not. Powerful – yes! I still have that book meant for children (see next page), but one that left this adult amazed once again at God's powerful presence in our daily lives. The worry that once gripped my life with fear had disappeared in a sea of heavenly love and reoccurring assurances that He was and remains right beside me every step of the way in my journey through life.

To close this chapter, I would like to briefly reflect on my brilliant light encounter in March of '93. After experiencing such an astounding event, one very significant connection I had unexplainably felt involved an interesting correlation between my awakening and the words of President George Herbert Walker Bush. In an inaugural speech on January 20, 1989, President Bush urged the citizens of the United States to replace costly government spending on poverty with volunteers, "… shining in the darkness like a thousand points of light." His repeated references to the points of light within our great country over the months and years following his inaugural message had taken on a monumental meaning in my life.

A heavenly messenger delivered this to our doorstep that late June evening.

Through my experiences, I envisioned a deeper understanding surrounding his words and the concept of which he spoke seemed more than just a casual reference to random individuals spreading their hope and goodwill throughout our society. Was it possible that George H.W. Bush had also experienced a personal encounter with "the light?" As the pilot of an Avenger Bomber in World War II, he and two other crew members were shot down on September 2, 1944, and miraculously the young future President was the lone survivor. While floating in the Pacific for several hours prior to the submarine U.S.S. Finback rescuing him, maybe this young airman was accompanied by a spiritual protector? Possibly, George H.W. Bush learned some of God's mysterious ways through the heroic yet traumatic experience thrust upon him for which he was awarded a "Distinguish Flying Cross" medal. If so, he theorized that certainly others had experienced similar occurrences in their lives. To this day, I wonder if there was any more significance to this common theme of lights or was it simply my misinterpreted sense of relevance. Only God and former President Bush know if any true connection existed.

Another interesting concept is my hypothesis that individuals experiencing high levels of mania are able to momentarily peer through the boundaries separating heaven and earth. Once my mind was expanded beyond earthly limits, often referred to as a "manic break" or a psychotic episode by psychiatric professionals, my heightened awareness of common surroundings and incidental events in life became very profound. I believe that a bipolar individual who becomes highly attuned briefly slips out of his or her spiritual shell causing the boundary between heaven and earth to become very thin like a veil. Many people would agree that God works in mysterious ways. Those of us who have experienced very elevated levels of mania may catch glimpses of His magnificent realm through the surly bonds which separate heaven and earth.

CHAPTER TEN
NORMALCY RETURNS

As the months passed after my mysterious encounter with the magnificent light, my mental faculties slowly and surely returned to a fairly normal state. With my ability to concentrate and focus improving every day, I was now able to actively return to my undergraduate studies and aggressively complete the degree program from Embry-Riddle for which I had originally enrolled some five years earlier. Having to complete just three courses during that Winter/Spring semester, I was extremely grateful to receive a "D" in MS 317 or Organizational Behavior. Up to that point, I had proudly completed all my college coursework earning A's and B's, and receiving such a sub-par grade before the onset of my illness would have caused me significant anguish. However, a below satisfactory grade in this challenging and highly subjective independent study course had seemed perfectly acceptable to me at this time.

Barely passing this upper level management science course allowed me to receive a diploma despite the devastating roadblocks presented during my highly manic state and ensuing depression in the months leading up to the final completion of my bachelor's degree requirements. I experienced a tremendous feeling of pride and a remarkable sense of accomplishment considering all the hardships and disappointments that were dealt to me over these years during my career development and pursuit of a college degree. I was elated and content to have completed the coveted prize that up until now, no one in my family had ever achieved. On May 30, 1994, nearly eleven years after graduating from the small rural Pennsylvania high school, I was awarded a Bachelor of Science degree in Professional Aeronautics. The Embry-Riddle Aeronautical University is one of the highest-rated and respected aviation institutions in the world and a degree from this prestigious university would considerably help my career.

After the successful completion of my degree program at age 29, I immediately began actively pursuing steady employment in the aviation field and was able to secure a position as a part-time Passenger Service Representative (PSR) for United Airlines at the Harrisburg International Airport. The employment opportunity with United was attractive because of the excellent benefits, including free travel and a comprehensive healthcare package even though the salary of the part-time PSR position was quite minimal. By working an additional job, driving limousines and shuttle van service for a local transportation company, I was able to supplement my income and our three lives began to return to some sort of normalcy.

With my mental health back and my once unraveled mind returning to its previous state of performance, I was again able to envision a successful life for my family. Although, at this point in time, it definitely appeared that my piloting career had finally come to a disappointing and unfortunate end of the road. I now aspired to the possibility of working my way up the corporate ladder into a flight operations management and/or pilot training position at one of the world's largest and most successful airlines. Being able to once again provide the financial support that would allow Andrea and I to regain our previously accustomed lifestyle, purchase a new home of our own and possibly have another child, was the dream I allowed myself to picture once again. However, little did I know that my wife of four years had now begun to doubt my ability to achieve my previous goals and to attain the visions that seemed to appear and then vanish before our eyes time and time again over the past few years.

Since my mental health progress was exemplary and my condition no longer required the attention it once did, I made a decision to have my psychological records and continuing care transferred to a new doctor. The new physician's office was closer to our apartment home in Mount Joy and the convenience of not having to drive nearly forty minutes to see Dr. Nutter would simplify my life. I asked Dr. Nutter to approve of my transferring to a local mental health clinic with an office located nearby in northern Lancaster County. He agreed that with my significant improvement and demonstrated stability it would probably be best to allow me to continue my treatment with a psychiatrist closer to where I lived. Dr. Nutter's care and patience to see me through my drastic up and down cycles was a real lifesaver. I was and remain extremely grateful to him for saving me from the depths of the darkness and bringing me back to reality when I was flying too high.

With my continued stabilization, he graciously and unselfishly transferred my care to another wonderful healer and trained caretaker of the mind. I met my new doctor, staff psychiatrist Dr. Theodore Kreizer, in the summer of 1994, and it was immediately apparent that this fine physician was a truly competent and uplifting professional. The compassion he showed coupled with tremendous medical expertise made him a real warrior in the mental healthcare field. Dr. Kreizer would eventually help me through some additional rough times that were currently just over the horizon, and he was very supportive in my pursuit to one day return to flying even though I was diagnosed with bipolar disorder.

He was an amazing doctor and I am extremely grateful for his talented capabilities in not only treating my inherited illness, but for providing the sensitivity of a caring counselor as well. From my vast experience, this unique combination of attributes in doctors is often missing in the somewhat rigid field of psychiatric treatment. Sadness overcame me on the day Dr. Kreizer advised me that he had obtained another career position and was moving his family back home to Indianapolis, Indiana, to pursue his new opportunity. Thank God for such excellent physicians!

> *"Thank you Dr. Kreizer for all the support and inspiration while under your outstanding care. Without a doubt, I am sure your brilliant light continues to radiate great hope and brings considerable comfort to the patients and the colleagues fortunate enough to be in your company. May you and your family be truly blessed..."*

While I was working long hours between the airport and my driving assignments at the limousine company, I made the greatest of effort to be the best husband and father I could possibly be. I cherished the time I was able to spend with my wife and son, but I began to sense that the vitality of our marital relationship was beginning to lose most of the remaining energy. Fortunately, by the late summer of 1994, my mental health was no longer a major factor as the continued lithium medication prescribed to control my genetic illness allowed me to lead a very regular and fairly normal life. At last I was feeling some sense of peace in my soul once again.

My mental wellness and stability were no longer questionable, but my marriage seemed to show signs of continuing wear. I was very disappointed in my conclusion that when it finally seemed I had turned the pages in chapters of my life that had previously contained the engulfing darkness, my wife was drifting uncontrollably away from me. Just when I felt uplifted on the road to a full recovery, Andrea's attitude and demeanor appeared to be bailing out of a situation that had been up to now somewhat of a "living hell" for her. I was deeply concerned as our marriage was slowly unraveling and seemed to be cracking at the seams just when I was truly learning to live again.

It was about this time that Andrea and a female co-worker had decided to pay a visit to a local fortune teller just as a different, exiting experience. She explained that they were going to this psychic just for kicks of sort, but not known to her, she was in for quite a surprise. After returning home from the meeting with this lady of fortune, as Andrea recanted what was communicated to her, I was emotionally moved and somewhat flabbergasted. This so-called psychic woman, supposedly a complete and total stranger, mysteriously looked deep into Andrea's soul, and her remarkable assessment of my wife was right on the money. This fortune teller told Andrea, "I can see and feel all the pain in your life brought about from your husband's serious health problems." Thankfully, she went on assuring Andrea of my devoted and unending love for her. She continued to explain the situation by saying, "If your husband were able to, he would reach up in the sky and capture a star for you." Andrea claimed to have brushed the majority of this psychic experience off as nonsense, but as she relayed the story to me, I could only marvel at the tremendous accuracy in the words of a total stranger as chills ran down my spine.

I continued to work a significant amount of hours to meet the financial demands of our family. Many nights I would work at the airport past midnight, cleaning the overnight aircraft and would not arrive home till the early hours of the morning. Often I would get up early to drive for the limousine service, and as the day progressed, the weight of my eyelids grew heavier as I struggled to stay awake behind the wheel. At times, I found myself driving in a very dangerous stupor, and I am extremely grateful and blessed that I did not have an accident while in these states of total non-alertness. My relationship with my wife continued to grow colder and colder as we drifted further apart. Conversation became strained, not responsive and physical contact was infrequent. I tried very hard to be kind, caring and attentive, but the spark that had brought us together several years ago and had grown into what I thought would be an eternal flame had seemed to be totally dowsed by the struggles of my illness over the last few years.

We were scheduled to take a greatly needed vacation in the early part of September, and after considerations of canceling and some serious discussions over finances, we decided to make the trip anyway in order to get away from all the anxiety and tension that had built up in our everyday lives. A few weeks later, upon our arrival in Rehoboth Beach, Delaware, the stress of our deteriorating relationship appeared to be somewhat relieved. We seemed to be enjoying life together as a family in the rented beach house as this was our only vacation in several years due to my mental health and financial difficulties. After getting Brydon off to sleep one night, during a rare, yet invigorating love-making experience, Andrea began to cry hopelessly for some unknown reason. She attempted to explain to me that she was tired of living the way we were living and stated that she felt that a separation was necessary as soon as possible. Perhaps Andrea had saved this inevitable news for our last night at the beach house because the emotions stirring inside her were ones she could no longer bare.

She stated, "Upon our arrival back in Mount Joy, I will be moving out!" I was shocked by the suddenness of this drastic revelation. Our marriage certainly had its problems, but a separation without any counseling whatsoever was not the best of actions and was unfathomable to me. After some lengthy discussions and convincing on my part, she agreed to attend a counseling session with me after we returned home, avoiding just moving out. I was somewhat encouraged by her change of heart, but certainly I knew the work that lay ahead was going to be a huge mountain to climb if our marriage would persevere. Through all the struggles and mental torment of my once debilitating illness, it was obvious that I still loved my wife dearly, and I remained totally committed to the vows we took four years earlier. I had always remained faithful to her and I believed the same of her. Little did I know at this time in our lives that she no longer shared our common beliefs nor walked the same faithful path. We both had changed.

Chapter Eleven
Unions Divided

After returning home from the beach vacation, we met with my psychologist for some emergency marital counseling. At the counselor's office in Elizabethtown, we discussed what had transpired while at the Delaware shore, and the goal of this first session was to avoid any rash decisions affecting the future of our marriage. After a one-hour session, calmer heads prevailed and we both agreed that we would maintain the status quo for at least two weeks and then reconvene to determine where things stood. Ironically, when Andrea returned home from work the next evening, she informed me that she had signed a lease on an apartment in Middletown and was definitely moving out. I was extremely perplexed and pretty distraught since she had promised to tough things out for a few more weeks in front of the counselor and me only the night before.

That weekend, my father and I helped Andrea move most of our furnishings including Brydon's personal belongings to her newly-leased apartment approximately fifteen miles north of where we had been living. I was pretty upset but tried to be supportive and helpful after concluding that maybe the time apart and some space between us would be beneficial. Possibly this separation she was intent on making happen could prove helpful in ultimately saving our strained marital relationship. However, my modest attempt at optimism would not last long. A few days after moving her into the new apartment, I would experience one of the biggest shocks of my life.

Often working at the airport into the early hours of the morning, I usually would sleep in until about 11:00 AM and was in bed sleeping a few days after my wife moved out when the doorbell rang. Being in a deep morning slumber, I initially ignored it. But after the doorbell continued to ring, I crawled out of bed, put on some clothes and slowly made my way from the bedroom to the front door. Upon opening the door, I was shocked awake and very surprised to see Andrea standing under the small awning of what was now my apartment. Normally, at this time of the day she would have been at work and I was totally caught off guard by her presence. She was obviously very upset and began crying uncontrollably as I invited her in. Her distraught behavior was due to the fact she was no longer able to conceal her darkest secrets and had stopped by to come clean with "the rest of the story."[18]

Several months ago, she began to develop a friendship with a man she had met through her work at the construction company and this friendship had developed into a much deeper relationship over time. She was able to confide her concerns and fears to him, and in my absence he provided a ready shoulder for her to cry on. Andrea was extremely vulnerable after dealing with my problems for so long and having experienced all the ups and downs of a rocky marital existence. I never learned the other man's identity, but in my opinion he took tremendous advantage of my wife during her darkest times in our marriage. Apparently he promised to give her a big house, more

---

[18] This saying is often attributed to Paul Harvey and his daily radio show which ends with such a titled segment

children and a life practically complete with silver spoons. When she moved out of our apartment, only then did he explain to her that he no longer desired her, because he knew she would eventually return to her husband. Apparently the conquest was over and he had suddenly turned her loose. Andrea came to see me that morning because she felt I deserved to know the reason for her leaving me so hastily, prior to her extramarital relationship crumbling.

I was dumbfounded at her news and had no idea that this affair had been going on behind my back for several months. The hurt was deeper than almost anything I had ever known, and a marriage which I felt should last forever, was in perilous jeopardy. We then talked and agreed it was best to again enter counseling in an attempt to sort out our emotions and to see if there was anything actually salvageable. I was initially reluctant to go into marital counseling after learning that the highest level of trust in our marriage had been breached; however, for our son's sake I agreed to see if we could find some common ground, mend the damage and possibly save our floundering relationship.

Andrea remained extremely upset during the first few sessions of counseling, trying to explain the reasoning behind her acts of infidelity but never showing any real remorse. As the counseling continued, I began to sympathize with her for looking outside our marriage for some emotional support. It was an understandable recourse as she had lived nearly two years of hell with a man afflicted with a debilitating illness that stressed our relationship beyond tolerable limits. Then she began to blame her unfaithful actions solely on me and never openly accepted responsibility for her immoral behavior that had shattered the institution of our marriage. After the finger-pointing continued in the sessions like a broken record, I finally reached my breaking point. At that time, I felt it prudent to discontinue any further marital counseling and decided to begin the process of filing for divorce. I theorized that a realistic threat of divorce might cause Andrea to open her eyes and take some responsibility for her actions. Shortly after I had served her with the divorce papers, she became involved with another man and my intention for the filing of divorce subsequently backfired.

In filing for the divorce, I hoped Andrea would be frightened into finally assuming responsibility for her actions. Furthermore, she would want to return to counseling so we could work through this major crisis in order to remain a family. Instead, the filing pushed her away and she sought comfort in the arms of another man. There were a few rays of hope for me left and occasional desires to reunite, but in the end, proceeding with the divorce seemed to be the most pertinent course of action. On May 23, 1994, our bonds of holy matrimony were legally dissolved by the courts. Andrea has since remarried to a very fine gentleman who has been a very positive influence on my son, Brydon. She recently told me that she is happy and I am grateful she has found the happiness I once longed to give her and which she so greatly deserves.

Overall, the trauma of a failed marriage and all the emotional roller coaster rides associated with my divorce had a big effect on my mental health. I remained on my medication and sought out psychological counseling to deal with the flood of emotions confronting me from all directions. In fact, I faired extremely well, never getting any lower than an occasional case of the blues. After a few months of counseling and after moving back into my parents' home for support, I had again returned to normal. Moving in with my folks was my only real option, because my erratic schedule included usually working early and late hours. I was able to keep Brydon, now two-and-one-half years old, with me nearly fifty percent of the time with these living arrangements. If I had to go to work early, he could sleep in and my Mom would be there with him when he rose in the morning. The opposite was true in the evening when Mom and/or Dad would get Brydon to bed when I worked past his bedtime. He would be comfortably asleep when I got home and served as a very pleasant alarm clock when the sun rose high enough in the sky to rouse him out of bed. I am extremely grateful to my parents for providing me a home where I could spend much quality time with my little boy. To this day, that special bond that developed between Brydon, his Pappy and his Grandma is very special.

Time marched on and in January 1995, my love life was pretty much non-existent. I had been saying fervent prayers for months asking God to bring someone into my life who could be a companion and to eventually allow a friendship that could prosper into something more. I had been able to put my divorce in the past and desired the opportunity to begin dating. Brydon would be three in February and most of my free time was spent being the best father I possibly could be. I purchased a golden retriever puppy for Brydon and myself, naming her B.G. which was short for her AKC registered name "Brydon's Girl." God bless my Mom who ended up spending the majority of the time taking care of my new little girl while I was at work. B.G. was a very rambunctious puppy and even with a complete obedience course under her belt, she was a true handful most of the time. Before she turned two, B.G. was adopted by a good friend of my Mom, for she had not had the opportunities at our house to get as much attention as an affectionate pup like she deserved. Initially, Brydon and I would go visit her once in a while and her new owner has always kept in touch and provided us with important updates about her well-being. On last report, B.G. is doing fine and she only started to mellow in her frisky ways when she turned eight years old.

On January 19th, I had stopped at a local Automated Teller Machine (ATM) to deposit my paycheck. I approached the ATM and needed a deposit envelope. I then proceeded to the front of the line and tapped the pretty young lady who was at the machine on the shoulder to request an envelope. Having several envelopes in my car, I had inconveniently forgotten to bring one with me. As I moved away from the front of the line and began to fill out the deposit information on a nearby counter, the attractive young woman approached me and asked if my name was Al Kent. Surprised that she knew my name, I answered that indeed it was and asked how she had known me. She explained that she went to high school with me and recognized me because I was a senior when she was a freshman. She told me her name was Brenda Johnson and we spoke briefly as I looked to see if she were wearing a wedding band. I saw a very thin gold band on her left ring finger, thus I deducted she was married. Brenda said goodbye and I headed to the ATM to make my deposit.

As I finished punching in my PIN number, I glanced over my shoulder to see this petite redhead with a quick laugh backing out of the parking spot. Our eyes met and with her tremendously intoxicating smile, she gave me a cute wave goodbye. My interest was truly peeked when my somewhat naïve reasoning deducted that a married woman would not have made such a friendly gesture while pulling away from the ATM. I was excited and felt like I was back in high school plotting my next move of first locating her and then asking her out. Brenda's last name was very common with literally hundreds of Johnsons in the phone book, and I was concerned that I might not be able to track her down again. Her youthful beauty and ear-to-ear smile made me committed to finding her phone number and somehow asking her on a date.

Where would my search to locate this intriguing freshman from my past who had piqued my interest during our brief ATM encounter begin? I started my search by giving my sister-in-law, Bobbie, a call to see if she could supply any information on Brenda's whereabouts, since

Brenda had literally captured my imagination at first sight. Bobbie and my brother were in the graduating class immediately behind Brenda's, and just maybe she could lead me in the right direction. Bobbie also was employed in the administrative offices at the high school that we all had attended. After a few days had gone by, I called Bobbie at the school offices and asked her about Brenda. Initially, she told me she knew who Brenda was, but she wasn't sure where Brenda lived or could not supply any additional information to help me locate her. After talking for a minute or two, Bobbie said, "Wait a minute!" As if a light bulb had suddenly come on, she remembered having seen Brenda's name recently as she grabbed a folder on her desk containing names of many individuals who had recently signed up for an adult education art course. Brenda and her sister had recently enrolled in the art class and my sister-in-law told me the information I so desperately desired was right there on top of the stack of completed forms. Wow, another one of those mysterious coincidences!

When I called Brenda, she remembered me from the ATM encounter and agreed to go out with me. Our first date involved taking Brydon to a children's comedy show featuring a good friend of mine from high school. We all had a great time and our relationship was "off and running." Our relationship continued to blossom as we began to get to know each other better. I knew Brenda was brought into my life for obvious reasons, as I have always held firm to the idea that everything is for a purpose. It was not long afterwards that I began to fall in love with this remarkable young woman, and after a year of dating, I asked Brenda to be my wife. I was overjoyed when she said, "Yes!" She was wonderful with Brydon and our loving relationship felt very close to perfect.

In October of 1995, I was able to gain employment as a part-time courier for FedEx™ in Lancaster, Pennsylvania. The financial compensation was greater and the benefit package was remarkable. I tried to work as much overtime as possible to supplement my income. While reviewing the company benefits guide, I noticed that financial assistance or tuition reimbursement was provided for certain types of training. One area of interest was flight training, and I looked into the possibility of getting an instructor's license for multi-engine aircraft. This was an important credential to acquire if I were to someday re-enter the airline industry as a flight simulator instructor and this advanced instructor rating was one that I had not obtained during my prior training.

After determining that Federal Express would indeed reimburse me for the expenses incurred while pursuing this new rating, I enrolled in a local flight school. After about a week of study and preparation, I spent the next week taking flight lessons from a qualified instructor in a small twin engine airplane successfully completing the multi-engine instructor course and passing my Federal Aviation Administration (FAA) check ride. This new rating on my Certified Flight Instructor license would allow me to do limited instruction in actual aircraft, but more importantly facilitate my ability to instruct in aircraft simulators, which was the preferred method of training at the larger air carriers.

Brenda and I continued to grow in our love for one another. Our engagement was rather jovial, romantic and fulfilling. Being unable to remember even one time of serious conflict or disagreement between us, I felt quite certain that I had finally met my soul mate. I considered our relationship a match made in heaven and looked forward to a lifetime of happiness with her. It was March 10, 1997, exactly sixteen years to the date of my brother's death, and I was staying the night at Brenda's apartment in Wyomissing, Pennsylvania. As we were asleep in the night, the bright overhead light in her bedroom suddenly illuminated. Being light sleepers, we both awoke immediately and wondered what happened to cause the light to come on. I glanced over my shoulder to see the light switch in the "OFF" position. Just then, the light extinguished. My fiancée and I lay in the dark bedroom, illuminated now only be the dim glow of street lights radiating through the curtains, talking about this mysterious event.

Brenda explained to me that she had sensed someone walking in the hallway and pictured a hand reaching into the room and turning on the overhead light switch. I cautiously got out of bed and searched the small one bedroom apartment but found no signs of lurking strangers or forced entries. As I lay back down in bed beside her, we discussed that it was the anniversary of my brother's death and talked about how my family and I had experienced similar phenomenon on this date in the past. These reoccurring and unexplainable events served as a reminder to me and now my wife to be that although Jeff was gone from this realm, his presence was never far away from us, especially on the tenth day of March.

After some thorough pre-marital counseling sessions with our pastor, Brenda and I were joined together in holy matrimony in September of 1997. Ironically, the ceremony took place in the same historical church of my first wedding. With our family and friends present, Brydon, now five, was my best man and life felt wonderful again. Our honeymoon was a marvelous trip to Vancouver, Canada, where we hopped a cruise ship headed southward for the ports of Seattle, San Francisco and Los Angeles. Brenda and I enjoyed the cruise immensely and the experiences on and off the large ship served as a magnificent beginning to our new life together.

I continued to take my medication, even though my bipolar diagnosis no longer had any detrimental effects on my day-to-day life. I was deeply in love with Brenda and with life and had a family unit back. Life was as normal as life can get. No, normal described my mental health condition, life was excellent! Shortly after our marriage, we purchased a new home in Denver, Pennsylvania, and settled into being a happy couple and concentrated our efforts on putting some money away to pursue future dreams. I was still working for Federal Express and Brenda was working in Berks County at an area women's shelter. Our relationship continued to prosper as the love we felt for each other seemed to grow stronger each day. I kept busy working around our new house and enjoyed the friendship we made with our surrounding neighbors. Everything was going quite well. Brenda was a great wife and stepmother to Brydon, and I felt a deep sense of happiness and contentment in my life.

Brenda had accepted a Continuing Medical Education (CME) Coordinator position at a large area hospital and I took on a second job working part-time at a local bank. I started as a teller and was later trained as a customer support specialist. My short tenure as a bank employee was quite interesting and allowed me to work with some great people at the small branch of a larger community bank. It was now 1998, and over four years had passed since I had experienced any more hardships and detrimental effects related to my bipolar diagnosis. I decided to make a serious attempt at re-certification with the Federal Aviation Administration (FAA) and applied for a special issuance medical certificate. Having applied previously and was subsequently denied, I was aware that the chances of my medical certificate being re-issued were slim, but I was still compelled to try again. A bipolar diagnosis and my dependency on lithium were considered a permanently disqualifying condition under current Federal Aviation Regulations. However, after several years of total stability and complete normalcy, I felt strongly that the FAA's blanket denial policy was discriminatory and unwarranted in my specific case. Furthermore, I was not willing to give up my aviation career without an aggressive fight.

A year earlier in 1997, I made a valiant attempt to convince the FAA Medical Certification Branch of my fitness to return to the cockpit and the career that I yearned to re-establish. Gathering and presenting substantial evidence would be necessary to convince FAA officials that bipolar disease actually could be stabilized as in my case and would not pose any threat to aviation safety. Shortly after my diagnosis was clarified and my stability was achieved, Dr. Nutter had notified me during one of my sessions of a study that was attempting to identify the gene or genes that cause bipolar disorder being conducted at the Johns Hopkins University Hospital in Baltimore, Maryland. I filled out the initial paperwork from the trade magazine copy supplied to me, and after Johns Hopkins personnel conducted some phone interviews, my family and I were accepted into this remarkable program that would attempt to unlock the secrets surrounding the hereditary links associated with this illness.

After speaking to several of the doctors I had come in contact with at Johns Hopkins, these caring medical professionals at this prestigious institution were sympathetic and agreed to help my personal cause in appreciation of my efforts to advance their important research work. I was very excited when a research assistant from Johns Hopkins called to notify me that they would be able to administer an independent psychiatric evaluation that I had requested in an effort to bolster my argument for re-certification with the FAA.

The arrangements had been made and on May 7, 1997, I arrived in Baltimore early in the morning and was put through a thorough and comprehensive battery of psychological testing that lasted well into the afternoon. The charge for this extremely valuable series of tests of my mental capabilities was nominal and the results would hopefully serve as the basis for my request to have my medical certificate re-instated with the Aero Medical Branch of the FAA. The final report was issued several weeks later, with copies being mailed to the FAA's medical branch in Oklahoma City, Oklahoma, to my attending physician and one to myself.

For the eleven different tests given to me, the results were glowing in nature, scoring above average in nearly every category. One test administered to me was a thorough examination of persistent attention, patterned after tests developed for use in the aviation and air traffic control fields, showed impressive results. A comprehensive psychiatric evaluation conducted by a board certified psychologist at one of the nation's premier medical institutions would certainly make the bureaucrats at the FAA see that although I took a medication to control an inherited disorder, my mental facilities were maintained and my ability to return to the piloting profession would not be impaired in any way. In his concluding remarks of the psychological evaluation, Dr. Edwards wrote:

> "There is no evidence in the examination of any compromise of intellectual or psychomotor function - including language, visuospatial organization, attention, concentration, memory, or fine motor speed and coordination - that might be related to Mr. Kemp's illness or its treatment. He appears to be quite normal in his mood as well, with no symptoms of depression, mania or hypomania."

After nearly six months, the decision I had feared once again was revealed in a denial letter from the FAA. My application was rejected without even acknowledging the Johns Hopkins comprehensive evaluation. I was very disappointed in their form letter of denial that I had seen several times before, and it was obvious that the time had arrived to seek legal counsel to possibly change existing regulations. I was in no financial condition to undertake an expensive legal proceeding against the "mighty" federal government, but after attempting to enlist the help of my U.S. Congressman and both of the Keystone State's Senators without any success, I had very few avenues left. If there was any chance of getting my career back, an attorney experienced in this specific field, would be essential to pressure the Federal Air Surgeon into putting aside pre-conceived bias, outdated medical analysis and discriminatory practices to focus on the facts regarding my case.

After researching legal precedence and case law surrounding my situation, I found that a legal argument very similar to mine was brought against the FAA several years ago. In this case, a plaintiff with bipolar disorder filed suit against the FAA and won his medical certificate back after the courts determined that his rights to pilot an aircraft were taken away without due cause. This individual was a private pilot from the Chicago, Illinois, area and I was a professional pilot requesting permission for the same accommodation to fly a commercial airliner. One evening, I picked up the phone and attempted a total "shot in the dark" by calling Chicago directory assistance and asking for this pilot's phone number.

I was pleasantly surprised when the directory assistance operator supplied me with his telephone number and was even more amazed that Bentley Rock answered on his cellular phone when I placed the call. After briefly explaining my situation, he was extremely cordial and very receptive to my plight. He told me a little about his case and informed me that his father handled his legal proceedings for him. Bentley's father, Gerald Rock, who owned a large law firm in Chicago, acted as his attorney throughout the legal action initiated against the FAA. After we talked for nearly thirty minutes, he told me to wait a couple of days and then to call his father at the number he supplied to discuss the possibility of his father helping me. He assured me that he would talk to his dad, give him my name and an overview of my situation. I thanked Bentley immensely and anxiously awaited my call to his father.

After a few days had passed, I was successful in contacting Mr. Rock and he spent a considerable amount of time talking to me on the phone. Gerald had been briefed, just as I had been promised, and he informed me that since their successful case, the Federal Air Surgeon's office had changed the regulations closing the loophole that proved fruitful in his son's case. The new regulations now contained specific language placing a blanket disqualification to fly for all individuals diagnosed with bipolar disorder. However, he offered me some encouragement and agreed to meet with me in his downtown Chicago office to further discuss my situation.

I wasted little time in setting the appointment and in early November 2000, I found myself aboard a flight from Harrisburg International to Chicago's O'Hare Airport. I took the train from the airport into downtown Chicago and upon exiting the underground station, I found myself right in the heart of the "Windy City". As I walked along the sidewalk surrounded by buildings that seemed to reach to the sky, I was very enthusiastic that this path might actually lead to a positive outcome. After a few blocks, I located the correct building and headed up several floors to meet Bentley's father. Gerald greeted me after a few minutes of waiting in the lobby, and I was immediately impressed with his warmth and genuine concern.

Gerald and I chatted for a while, and I learned that he was a pilot as well, very experienced and committed to general aviation concerns in the local community. His efforts to keep the historical Meigs Field in downtown Chicago open spanned many years prior to the eventual defeat of politically motivated airport wrecking crews. Although his large law firm specialized in patent rights, he had himself taken the fight to the FAA because of his aviation knowledge and his concerns for the rights of his son.

We continued to discuss my situation and his son's case over lunch and he agreed to take on the responsibility of researching the specifics pertinent to my case and of preparing a comprehensive legal brief outlining the legal arguments we could put forward and examining my chances of success. He would need to secure a $2,500 retainer fee to undertake this initial ground work. I left Chicago that day very impressed with Gerald and only had to decide if I was willing to make this significant financial investment in hopes of suing to regain my beloved career. I told Gerald that I would need a few days to think about his proposition and I would call him soon with my decision.

My thoughts were pretty focused on getting this legal process started and it took very little self-convincing to arrive at my decision. After arriving home and discussing the issue with my wife, she was fully supportive of my decision to send Gerald a retainer fee and pursue a legal course of action in an attempt to reverse the discrimination I had perceived the FAA imposed on me. I decided to take the funds out of my retirement plan with tax penalties and all and next made the call to have Gerald begin his investigation and represent me in this complicated and drawn-out process. I now had an attorney and felt a glimpse of hope in this major uphill battle.

After several months of supplying significant documentation to Gerald and his team, the legal brief and summary had been completed. It was a fairly comprehensive seven-page document describing the basis for possible stances and legal arguments. It offered some hope, but was cautiously optimistic stating that this would be a major fight with no guarantee of a positive outcome. The FAA would make repeated motions to dismiss the case causing it to be tedious and expensive. Gerald agreed to pursue my case aggressively but stated that he would need at least $40,000 up front to start the complicated process. I certainly did not have funds of this amount available and was not willing to take out a second mortgage with the chance of losing the case and having such a huge debt to pay off with nothing to show. After being enthusiastic and upbeat about my new legal representation, the cruel reality of my insufficient financial situation and the lack of funds to mount a legal assault against the FAA stood as a major roadblock in my pursuit of justice. In desperation, I sent a letter explaining my entire situation to Mr. William Gates, founder of Microsoft™ and the Gates Foundation, requesting support for my plight and with hopes of receiving some financial assistance in my fight against the perceived discrimination of this branch of the federal government. No response or reply was ever received from that long-shot correspondence asking for help sent on a wing and a prayer.

In the fall of 1998, through my employment at the bank, I had run into an individual from my past at a nearby fast food restaurant. Kim Peony had been the head flight attendant at the first airline I had worked for and was now the manager at a local McDonald's™. I was surprised to hear that she had married a former co-worker of mine and that her husband, Fred, was still with the airline some eleven years later. I would stop by her restaurant regularly during my breaks while shuttling between jobs, and a few times we were able to talk a short while. I briefly explained how I had lost my medical certificate because of a serious sleep disorder requiring medication and how I desired to return to gainful aviation employment possibly in a flight training position.

Kim offered to give my résumé to her husband and would ask him to see if the airline was in need of anyone with my experience and background. Her husband had previously served in the training department but currently was the Director of Systems Control. Shortly after Fred carried in my résumé, I received a call from the Director of Training, stating that he was currently looking for an instructor to teach ground schools for newly hired pilots, and an interview was arranged. I was excited at the prospect of returning to the airline in a training capacity and also to a company where I knew many of the key individuals and a significant number of pilots I had flown with in years past.

On the day of the interview, I was totally surprised as the Director of Training, Charles Webber, whom I had met several years before while trying to find local aviation employment, clearly remembered me and my situation regarding the loss of my FAA medical certificate. He continued the interview by handing me a sheet of paper that contained the specific job description of this new position. He explained what he would expect of me in the instructor position which I now began to understand was tailored for me if I agreed to accept his offer. We completed our meeting that day with the mutual understanding that the job was mine for the taking only having to iron out an initial salary level and determining when I would start. A few days later, Charles called me with a confirmed offer of employment after we agreed on a salary and an official start date. On January 3, 1999, just prior to my 34th birthday, I started my new instructor position at the small regional carrier based in Middletown, Pennsylvania, not far from the Harrisburg International Airport. I was elated to be back in the aviation arena, one that I had known and loved for years, and instructing was a job I would grow to eventually love.

My commute to work was over one hour each way, but Brenda still worked in the Reading area. We would have to continue living in our home in Denver which offered convenience to her work in Berks County and also provided easy access to the turnpike for my westbound commute each morning. A few months after reestablishing my career track and with my job going exceptionally well, Brenda began to search for employment opportunities in the Harrisburg area. She eventually interviewed and accepted a position at a sexual assault agency located in the capital city area. We now began to commute together each day and besides saving money on gasoline, the two-three hours of daily travel were quite invigorating and allowed us to solidify our marriage even further. After several months of our enjoyable commutes and healthy conversations, Brenda and I decided to begin the process of house hunting in the Harrisburg area.

About the same time we started thinking about relocating to the capital city region, we had decided to buy a new automobile for our lengthy weekday commutes. Brenda's 1986 Corolla was showing serious signs of aging, and we found an attractive deal on a nice 1993 Accord EX from a local used Honda™ dealer. The dark green, five-speed Accord was a remarkable vehicle and we often argued, nicely of course, over who would drive it during our commute each day. As a general rule, in the morning I drove to my work and she would drive on to her office. Brenda would return to pick me up in the afternoon, and I would drive us home. This way we both were able to spend some time behind the wheel of our exciting new vehicle.

One evening while returning home from our daily commute, as we drove eastbound on Route 283 toward Lancaster, the Accord that we had admired suddenly lost power shortly after passing the Spooky Nook exit. As we decelerated to a crawl along the shoulder of the highway, I made several attempts to restart the engine. Creeping to a halt, it was obvious that our newly-purchased automobile was out of commission. After placing a call to the American Automobile Association (AAA) emergency road service and waiting nearly an hour for the tow truck to arrive, Brenda brought to my attention that it was March 10, 1999, the anniversary of my brother's untimely death back in 1981. Once again, we were left to discuss another interesting situation about still another mysterious occurrence happening on the tenth day of the third month.

Once the wrecker driver arrived on the scene, he made several unsuccessful efforts to start the car, also. After hooking us up to the tow truck, he pulled us to Marty's Garage near Schaum's Corner, the place where we had purchased the Accord. The owner and proprietor of this small establishment is probably the greatest Honda™ mechanic in the world. He and his wife run an excellent and respected automobile sales and repair shop. From my cell phone, I called Marty to notify him of our situation and warn him that we were being towed in. When we pulled into his place of business, and I do mean "pulled,"[19] Marty dropped everything to attend to our disabled vehicle and get us back on the road under the car's own power. Surprisingly, once the tow truck driver dropped the front end of the car to the ground, Marty jumped in and started it right up. In my opinion, he possessed the "Midas touch" with an automobile that had been down for the count, somehow convincing our Accord to come back from the dead.

He drove our vehicle into the repair bay and explained how sometimes electronic modules go bad and how he had replaced many of them before selling us the car. As we waited, he insisted on changing the remaining components to ensure we would not be stranded again. The time needed and parts required to repair our car would have cost several hundred dollars; however, he charged us nothing and we never experienced another problem again. The beloved Accord met an untimely death and was totaled when I was rear-ended on the Washington, D.C., beltway in 2002. This vehicle was purchased originally "as is" and cost

---

[19] Brenda and I rode in the elevated car behind the AAA tow truck for nearly ten miles and had an interesting time taking in the sites as we left the driving to someone else.

us a little over ten thousand dollars, but the integrity and righteousness shown by Marty and his wife were priceless.

By the summer of 1999, we decided to make the move to Harrisburg. We listed our home in Denver and found a nice, affordably priced, two-story home in Susquehanna Township near Linglestown. We made an offer on the home in a subdivision called Brandywine Estates, and luckily received a contract on our Denver home shortly thereafter. We closed on our home in Denver in the morning and drove to Mechanicsburg to close on the new house the same afternoon. The move went smoothly and we were content with our new home and our significantly shorter commutes to work.

At this point in my life, all was going quite well. My marriage continued to strengthen and I loved Brenda with all my heart. Nearly everything in our relationship felt perfect and literally I could have not asked for anything else in life. I was one hundred percent content and had a beautiful wife who was truly "the love of my life."[20] My career was finally back on track, I felt like I had a very satisfying and fulfilling marriage, and I was able to be a quality father to my son with tremendous support from my wonderful wife. Brenda would often take Brydon to the library and was just a model stepmother who provided him and me with a cohesive family unit that we had not had for quite some time.

Prior to our marriage, we had not planned on having any additional children of our own. Being positive influences in Brydon's life and lending him the parental support he needed to make his life whole were the only child-rearing objectives we had envisioned. Both Brenda and I had deep concerns about bringing another child into a world filled

---

[20]   The country song, "The Love of My Life" performed by Sammy Kershaw was a popular song on the radio during this time and I would often pretend to perform, lip synching the words especially for her when we heard it together.

with so much chaos and increasing problems. When the subject was discussed a few years later, our new pastor explained his interesting viewpoint. By creating a new life, our offspring would serve as a candle providing a small but needed light in a world we both perceived to be quite dark. The seed our pastor had planted in our hearts began to take root and as our love for each other continued to grow, Brenda became more and more interested in the possibility of motherhood. After some serious discussions, we agreed to begin trying for a little brother or sister for Brydon.

Shortly after the 2000 New Year, we aggressively scheduled our romantic rendezvous in an attempt to start a new little life borne of our love for one another. This time of sharing my entire being with the woman I loved so much was certainly one of the best periods in my entire life. By April of that year, our valiant and enjoyable efforts had proved to be successful as we learned of our pregnancy. It was an amazing feeling to go through this expectant period as a whole person while not being suffocated by the darkness which was present in my life during the pregnancy of my first child. The joy and happiness I experienced in the months following the conception made up for the fear and anxiety that gripped my life during the time in which my first wife Andrea was carrying our son Brydon. This time around, I was able to attend Lamaze classes with my loving wife while looking forward to and preparing for the birth of our child.

On January 8, 2001, a little boy named Alex Shea Kent was born to us. He arrived into this world just before 5:00 PM and was truly a precious bundle of joy. While assisting in the birth and experiencing Alex's arrival up close and personal, I was once again overcome with tremendous emotion. I cried with great joy while participating in this magnificent event and the tears of happiness flowed uncontrollably. Without a doubt, the births of my two sons have been dual zeniths in my life. In these most joyous moments, actually seeing one's own flesh and blood entering into the world is miraculously astounding. Brydon, who was about to turn nine, welcomed his little brother Alex into our lives with great interest. It was funny during the pregnancy when he thought we were just kidding him about having a sibling. As Brenda's midsection began to expand, he knew something was changing, but at his young age he was still a little reluctant to face the fact that a little baby would be joining our family soon. As he held his new little brother for the first time, it was now obviously apparent that he did indeed have a brother to love and be an important role model. We were all happy to welcome Alex into our lives.

Brenda decided to take three months maternity leave from her job and she was able to stay home with Alex during his early days. It was a wonderful experience coming home to both of them after work each day, and when the time had come for my wife to return to work, I was able to take a 90-day leave of absence from my work under the auspices of the Family Leave Act. Fortunately, we were able to swing the finances for me to be off for an extended period, and this time enabled me to stay home with my newest son for the next few months. The time I spent with Alex was very enjoyable and quite fulfilling. Spending quality time together at this early age helped create a very special bond between him and me that still exists today.

We were able to arrange suitable daycare for Alex in a wonderful lady's home as the time approached for my return to work. Having been introduced to Kay Nye at church, she would be Alex's caregiver Monday through Friday as both Brenda and I normally worked regular business hours during the week. Shortly after my return to work, it was apparent the honeymoon and the fairytale marriage we had up to this point had begun to lose its once glimmering shine. Our love for Alex was strong and steady, but our love for each other seemed to begin drifting away.

Brenda's work began to take on an ever increasing role and my role as a significant other began to take on a diminishing role. Brenda usually took Alex to the babysitter's in the morning, and I would pick him up on my way home from work. Many evenings after picking Alex up at Kay's, we would arrive home, get settled in and I would start supper only to learn when Brenda called that she was still working long after her scheduled work day should have ended. When I asked her to attend more to the needs of her family and the responsibilities she now had at home, she would get very defensive. We drifted farther and farther apart with arguments daily as the unpleasant struggle between her vocation and her new role as a mother caused increasing strain on our once stellar relationship. I thought, "Please, God, not again."

While my marriage was experiencing difficulties, my career was going rather well. After instructing pilot ground schools for nearly two years, the decision was made to have me fully trained on the aircraft I had been teaching. Although I still had not received medical clearance to fly, I would be checked and qualified as if I were to serve as a Captain for our regional airline. I traveled to Charlotte, North Carolina, and went through several weeks of intensive flight training accomplished in a full-motion simulator. At the completion of the training course, I successfully passed my check ride with a company designated examiner and an FAA inspector observing my piloting skills and decision-making abilities. I earned an Airline Transport Pilot's license and a DHC-8 Type, a specific rating required to act as pilot-in-command on this particular aircraft. Feeling very proud of my accomplishment, I was also extremely grateful to my boss, Charles, for helping me attain this highest level of qualification in the piloting profession.

We scheduled a needed family vacation to Wildwood Crest, New Jersey, during the second week of September 2001. Brydon, Alex, Brenda and I would spend some quality time, resting and relaxing at the Jersey shore and although our marriage was showing recent signs of fatigue, our vacation got off to a good start. While Brydon and I were riding bicycles on the boardwalk on a bright sunshiny and cloudless Tuesday morning, September 11th, little did we know that the world was beginning to unravel somewhat around us and that the terrible events of that day would change the world forever.

As we arrived back to our hotel room, Brenda had the television turned to CNN and shouted to us that an airplane had crashed into the World Trade Center (WTC). My first thought was what size plane had hit the horrifying smoking tower I was viewing on the TV screen, and I asked Brenda what else they were reporting. As she was telling me that the only information available was that a twin engine plane had hit the WTC south tower, I watched in a state of shock as I saw a large airliner suddenly appear into the live television picture. As it streaked across the sky from right to left and smashed directly into the second WTC tower, my mind could not comprehend what my eyes had just witnessed! Realizing shortly thereafter that what I had just seen was a large commercial aircraft being used as a weapon of mass destruction, I was speechless and frightened that more terrorist acts would follow to harm our country and many innocent citizens. The initial devastation that occurred that morning and the ensuing collapse of both WTC towers were incomprehensible to all of us.

My family watched in amazement, shock and sorrow as the events of the infamous day continued to unfold. I was affected deeply, having been in aviation, this tragedy seemed to hit those of us in the airline industry extra hard. My emotions were stirred vigorously and I was compelled to call my parents to tell them how much I cared for them and that we were shaken by the tragedies but physically alright. For me, the world turned upside down that September morning, and the importance of family and friends during such chaotic times was solidified to the highest degree. I am firmly convinced that each day is a gift from God, and we must cherish those we love because one never knows the time or the place that our earthly existence could abruptly end. Leaving the Jersey shore at the end of that tragically memorable week, I was recommitted to the loved ones in my life and would never again take our freedoms and liberties in this great country for granted.

After what was intended to be a relaxing vacation, we returned to our home in Harrisburg late Saturday evening following that emotionally-draining week. I was totally shocked when Brenda told me she was going to go into work the next day. Even though it was Sunday, she wanted to get caught up on the work she had missed while we were on vacation and to get a head start on the activities that lay in the week ahead. I could not believe what I was hearing after a week of terror and witnessing "hell on earth" for our country. I then realized how short life can be and how important family was and still is. At a time when most Americans rallied around family, friends and their faith, Brenda could only focus on going back to work early, on a Sunday for God's sake. This experience created a lasting memory that drove a decisive wedge between us that would eventually lead to the unworkable reconciliation of our diverging souls.

I am reminded of her actions whenever I hear the song titled "Where Were You" by country singer Alan Jackson. Jackson's song, a tribute to the September 11th tragedy, starts out by saying, "Where were you when the world stopped turning?" The ballad tells of individuals doing very sentimental things including holding hands with strangers, praying in church, calling loved ones or just breaking down and crying. When I hear this very emotional song today, while most people were cherishing what in life meant the most to them, I think of my wife leaving her family and finding refuge at her place of work. I could not believe her actions then, but I now have some understanding as to why she felt the need to wrap herself up in her career to the point of alienating a husband who once loved her more than anything in the world.

I was now trapped in an unbelievable nightmare. Our once perfect marriage lay broken and tattered before my very eyes. After Alex was born, Brenda continued to seem very disinterested in romance. Even many months after normal healing processes from giving birth were completed, she possessed little or no desire to engage in what was once very passionate and fulfilling intimacy. Now, nearly eight months after the birth of our child, any physical and loving contact between the two of us was non-existent. I attempted to initiate her affection, however, to no avail. I could no longer remember the last time we had shared intimate relations, even romantic tendencies and signs of affection had disappeared from our floundering marriage.

I insisted that she seek professional help, and after several months of physical rejection and hesitation, she agreed to enter counseling. After several months of Brenda seeing a counselor, I saw no signs of progress and when I would ask her how the sessions were going, she would simply say that everything was going okay. By now our relationship was truly plutonic and I could not conceive how our marriage made in heaven had turned into such a farce. Rejection of my love and affection was a heavy blow, although I still loved Brenda and remained committed to her in the marriage but was totally frustrated by her lack of concern for us.

We remained fairly civil to each other and talked quite regularly, but when I would ask her about her counseling, she would tell me nothing hopeful. I told her I wanted to go to a session or two of counseling with her and she was adamant against me going with her. She would say that the majority of the problems she possessed were in her head and she had to work through them alone. The anger began to build up inside me as she would often act like nothing at all was wrong, even though our relationship no longer had any intimacy whatsoever. Upon pressing her for answers as to why, she told me one evening in a very nonchalant manner that she could not envision us ever making love again. I was stunned and completely devastated. The woman that I loved and who promised to be my wife "till death do us part" no longer wanted any part in the greatest form of communication shared between a husband and a wife.

Finally, I pressured her into telling me just what was occurring in the counseling sessions she had been in for many months and pleaded for her to stop excluding me by letting me come along to a session or two. Again she denied my request and refused to allow me to be a part of her secretive counseling efforts. I was finally able to get her to divulge these two bits of information to me. Brenda said, "My counselor told me to tell you that I am really sorry for putting you though this difficulty, and in order to be a good mother to Alex, I must be a working mother." Several months of counseling and this is all I was to receive? I reasoned Brenda wasn't sorry, her counselor told her to tell me she was sorry for putting me through this aggravation and I did not even have the slightest idea of the root of this difficulty. My total frustration began to breed increased anger as I was running out of patience each day. We would begin to argue more and talk less as the tension in our house grew to intolerable levels. I never physically or verbally abused Brenda, but my unhappiness at her rejection and my escalating anger toward her dictated a separation.

In July of 2002, eighteen months after Alex was born, I took a new job in the Washington, D.C., area and moved out. We discussed the move and agreed it was for the best. Possibly our being apart would help relieve the incredible tension we both were feeling and the distance and time away from each other might help us get through these rough times. I had little hope that after a separation we might rekindle any remaining feelings we had for each other. I was extremely doubtful of reconciliation but because of the pleasant memories of times past, I held on to the sliver of hope that this desperate situation might be miraculously rescued. I certainly did not want to lose Brenda, our marriage and our family unit.

After three months of employment in Northern Virginia near Dulles Airport, the weekends I would stay at home with Alex and my wife did little to cure the serious problems of a withering marriage. Upon asking her, Brenda informed me that she had stopped seeing her personal counselor and refused to even consider the possibility of us entering marriage counseling together. She became quite independent of my presence and began to attend Sunday services at a local Unitarian Church. Having met many of her friends from work who were openly homosexual, I figured that she had found a new and alternative lifestyle, and I back pedaled from a situation that was increasingly confusing. Totally exasperated by her, frustrated and almost lost, I turned the entire situation over to God and prayed fervently for Brenda to return to the woman I had married over four years earlier.

It was fairly obvious our marriage stood very little chance of survival as Brenda and I were headed in opposite directions. I accepted a new employment opportunity as a Pilot Training Supervisor in Pittsburgh, PA, and I gave Brenda one last chance to save our marriage. I asked her sincerely to move with me to western Pennsylvania, get into counseling together, stay at home for a while raising Alex and just maybe we could triumph over our hardships and ultimately become a family again. She declined the offer giving no indication about her real reasons for ending our relationship. Soon our home north of Harrisburg went up for sale as I made the migration to the western part of the state alone.

It wasn't long before our house was sold and I moved into an apartment in Moon Township, PA, and Brenda moved to an apartment complex not far from where we had once lived. Alex had been enrolled in an excellent Christian daycare. Although it was hard to leave him, I knew that between the daycare, his mother and with the Lord watching over him he would be fine. I still had some lingering hope for our marriage but knew it would take a miracle to mend the broken fences. As we went our different ways, it was quite ironic that divorce had not been mentioned up to this point. I prayed for her, still my true love, and wished for a miracle each and every day for all of us.

As I began my new position as an Instructional Supervisor for an emerging regional airline, I totally engrossed myself in my job duties and responsibilities. I worked extremely hard and did not want loneliness to set in. Amazingly, through the craziness in my waning marriage and the separation from my family, my mental health remained fairly stable. I did have some trouble expressing the frustrations that I felt and often some anger would build up inside, but for the most part, I never got down on myself and was doing remarkably well. After nearly a year of living the status quo, the situation began to drag my spirits down. Even with my medication, I began to have some difficulty obtaining a good night's sleep. Increased pressures at work, coupled with the dismal uncertainty of my marital situation were starting to cause some problems in my day-to-day activities.

I decided to get some help, so one day I picked up the phone and called the Employee Assistance Program (EAP) through work to enroll in some counseling sessions. Hopefully, the sessions would allow me to find some relief from the great deal of anxiety and impending stress I was feeling from my confusing circumstances. The EAP personnel made an appointment for me to see a female counselor located by Station Square just west of downtown Pittsburgh. When I met Kimberly May for my first session, I was relieved that I had taken the initial step to get help and maybe find some closure to a very delicate marital situation I was not ready to give up, yet.

At my first session with the counselor, I shared my frustration regarding my failing marriage and discussed the many issues that led to the deterioration of such a once wonderful relationship. As I related the stories surrounding our marriage, Kimberly began to suspect something that had never even crossed my mind before this evening. I explained to her how once Alex was born, Brenda grew to become rather distant to me and how she would shy away from any attempts of intimacy and affection. I told her about how at times my wife would no longer allow me to touch her in normally erotic areas, even before our son was born. I thought this behavior was quite strange because during our courtship and into our initial years of marriage, our love life was vibrant and virtually unlimited in scope.

I also told my counselor about Brenda's worst experience, one she had related to me while at a high school slumber party. With many of her female friends sleeping around her, one boy crawled into her sleeping bag and forced himself upon her as she lay powerless, freezing in the face of fear from his unwanted advances. As this sexual predator stole the innocence of my wife to be, she was so traumatized and paralyzed, that she was unable to alert her friends of the terrible violation happening to her body and innocence. It was extremely difficult for me to understand how this could have happened without her screaming out and awakening her nearby friends. When recalling this horrendous experience from her teenage years, Brenda told me that she wanted to cry for help, but her body became completely lifeless and her desperate internal pleas went unheard as her voice was frozen by fright.

At this point, Kimberly interrupted my recanting of this dreadfully painful experience and proceeded to offer a plausible explanation of what she believed had happened to my wife. I was relieved to hear that her frank explanation of why Brenda had checked out on our marriage and what had caused her distant attitude toward me was forthcoming.

Kimberly used her many years of experience in counseling to explain to me that from all that I had been communicating to her pointed to the following conclusion. Brenda's inability to call for help at the slumber party was a definite sign that she had probably been sexually abused earlier in life, most likely as a young child when she was much too young to know how to handle the situation. The repressed memories of these childhood nightmares were most likely released when she gave birth to our son.

My counselor informed me that is was quite common for sexually abused women to suffer flashbacks and memory recollections resulting from the tremendous amount of hormones given off during childbirth. I asked myself if this were simply a case of an off-base counselor with a "Freudian" view trying to explain my wife's strange behavior as a result of imaginary childhood molestations. As we continued to discuss this issue, the evidence she put forward fully supported her hypothesis, and I became convinced beyond a reasonable doubt that my wife was truly a victim of this senseless early-childhood victimization.

I began to feel extremely sympathetic and compassionate toward Brenda and guilty of not seeing these signs of the perceived haunting ordeal earlier in her life. I became extremely emotional as my feelings for my wife turned to total concern, and yet a sense of relief and a small spirit of hopefulness overcame me simultaneously. My eyes had been opened to the apparent reasons for her secrecy and for not allowing me into the counseling process. The nightmare Brenda had been living was apparently too traumatic to share with anyone, and I felt great pain for her as the truth of the matter had seemingly been revealed, finally. With this new information, maybe our marriage could be salvaged after all. After a few more counseling sessions, Kimberly encouraged me to send Brenda a short letter telling her I had learned her darkest secret.

She provided the insight and basically dictated the words for me to use in this brief memorandum. The letter went something like this...

Dear Brenda,

I now know why you are sorry for putting me through "this ordeal." Your secret is safe with me, but when you are ready to divulge your darkest memories, I will be here to help you through all of "this." You are the victim here and I'll pray for you always.

Your Loving Husband,

Al

I called Brenda's older sister, Carol, and related that I needed to talk with her in private as soon as possible. We arranged a meeting at a Red Lobster™ restaurant in southwestern Pennsylvania halfway between my place and her home in Garrett County, Maryland. After laying out the whole picture and presenting the pieces of the puzzle surrounding the counselor's hypothesis, she agreed that the evidence made for quite a compelling case. Carol concurred that something horrifying must have happened in Brenda's early years involving men, because this apparent early life trauma seemed to have guided Brenda's entire life in a direction that involved serving the needs of women. Looking back after graduating from college, Brenda attended graduate school, receiving a master's degree in Women's Studies. She went on to work as a counselor in two women's shelters and served as a medical coordinator for a rape crisis agency. This career history of Brenda's further validated the theory that she was indeed a victim, dedicating her life to ensure that other women would not have to experience the same pain she had experienced, pain that remained trapped deep inside her. My counselor warned me not to get my hopes raised too high, as I had a rough road ahead of me with no guarantee that our relationship had not already reached the point of no return.

When Brenda received my short letter, she was totally perplexed as to what it meant and why I had sent it. She explained she had no idea what secrets I was referring to and I am quite sure she began doubting whether or not my mental capacities were still fully intact. I was completely shocked by her reaction. When I was able to discuss this issue in detail with her face-to-face, I told her everything about piecing together the evidence and how my counselor and I came up with the theory that she was sexually abused as a child and how her abuse was the root of her pushing me away. As a trained professional in the sexual assault field, she was in agreement that the facts I presented did make for interesting support of our theory. However, she denied having any recollection of any abuse in her life and could not accept the fact that these repressed memories, if indeed they actually existed, had anything to do with her current feelings and lack of marital commitment. The answers I thought I had derived and the hope I envisioned suddenly vanished as Brenda communicated her inability to remember any improprieties from her early years.

After a few more counseling sessions, I was able to find some peace as both Kimberly and I agreed that Brenda was possibly hiding her deepest feelings to protect her vulnerability. We surmised that while in counseling for many months, apparently Brenda uncovered the tip of a very large iceberg which was her childhood abuse, and it scared her tremendously. Visiting these repressed memories was simply too painful, so she ran from the truth that might have exposed everything, instead she locked the secrets away in a heavily-guarded vault. In my opinion, my wife was indeed violated as a child and I pray that one day she can get the personal help she deserves with this very complicated situation.

Several months later after reaching some inner peace and discontinuing counseling, I put forward one last valiant effort by writing an emotionally outpouring letter to my wife shortly before Thanksgiving (dated November 24, 2003). This final letter was composed after much deep thought and profound prayer...

Dear Brenda,

I have gone to great extents searching for answers trying to figure out how our relationship went from a marriage made in heaven to the sad state it is today. When I met you, I was sure God brought you into my life for definitive reasons. Our courtship was very enjoyable and satisfying, and I had no doubts when I asked you to marry me. During the first few years of our marriage, I felt that you were a guardian angel sent to help make my life whole again and you did. When we said our vows to each other; we both promised a lifetime commitment to "us" and the children that our love would produce. I have tried to be a productive participant in resurrecting our love, but I honestly feel that you have abandoned the promises you made before God, our relatives and our friends. I am no Saint, but know I am a very good man, a great father and tried my best to be a loving husband. Forgive me if I sound modest, but I don't think you realize the magnitude of what you are throwing away.

The issues facing us are numerous, but I would like to focus on the two main issues I see have caused our relationship to go astray. First is your very serious sexual dysfunction. When I met you, you were dating a man that treated you badly and did not know the meaning of affectionate physical relations (from what you told me). I attempted to show you the true meaning of "Making Love" and how sexual relations between two loving adults should be. A marriage needs affection and intimacy to be whole and we had that for some time. Making love between a husband and a wife is supposed to be a tender, pleasurable and enjoyable experience. Most healthy individuals have normal desires and needs that only a loving marital relationship can fulfill. You no longer seem to have these needs.

*I am convinced beyond a shadow of a doubt and from my counseling experience that you were sexually abused as a child, thus explaining your total lack of a physical commitment to the man you promised to stand by forever. After Alex's birth, the internal time bomb was activated and a terrified and stifled Brenda came into being. I don't blame you for this; **you are the victim** here. Please understand that with aggressive professional help, the full affects of the bomb may still be diffused if you're willing to attack it head on. I will continue to pray for you because I am afraid you may never be able to come to grip with your situation.*

The second issue I would like to point out is my perception of your selfishness. I realize that accepting the above conclusion seems unfathomable and is probably very frightening, but through this you have given little or no consideration to the affect it has had and will continue to have on others in your life. You told me early on that the problems you were experiencing were "all in your head" and that you were sorry for putting me through this. You refused to discuss with me the content of your counseling sessions and were adamant against us going into counseling together. Most couples enter counseling before throwing a marriage away, especially when children are involved. Currently, to my knowledge, you are not in counseling to attempt to address your problems that not only affect you, but also affect the lives of Alex, Brydon and I. In addition to our failing relationship, Alex has the right to know the meaning of a family and to be raised under one roof by two parents that love him. On our present course, it is apparent he will have little or no memory of a "family concept".

I want you to know that I have remained true to you throughout this long ordeal, but my love for you is dwindling. I wanted to remain overnight at your apartment more often to have additional time with Alex and maybe work on what little hope still exists. It is apparent that you don't feel the same way. I am requesting once and for all an honest answer. Are you willing to put forth the effort, face the challenges of addressing your problems and get the serious help you need in an attempt to salvage our relationship? I will stand by you and support you with all my heart and soul if you chose to fight these demons that have stolen the life from the young woman I fell in love with over eight years ago. Take some time to seriously think about what I have written, but I would appreciate the courtesy of a reply to this letter. Until we talk....

Love, Al

After three months had come and gone, I had received no response whatsoever to my soul-bearing correspondence. By asking her directly, I confirmed that she had indeed received the letter, and her silence left me deeply wounded and utterly speechless. After nearly two years of separation and misconceived hopes of reconciliation, it was obvious that Brenda had already emotionally divorced me, and the ball was now in my court to bring this sorry situation to an end. The time had come for me to take the necessary legal actions to have our shattered marriage dissolved. I filed for divorce and after the mandatory waiting period in a no-fault divorce had passed, in August 2004, a marriage that originally felt like it was made in heaven was legally dissolved by the laws of the Commonwealth of Pennsylvania.

CHAPTER TWELVE
LIFE GOES ON

After the stress of my second marriage having failed somewhat subsided, I settled into a calming realization that I could and must achieve happiness on my own. For several years, I had been trying to lead a life focused on pleasing my spouses and helping them achieve their dreams while failing to recognize my own personal aspirations. I was able to purchase a townhouse in Imperial, Pennsylvania, and having my own place turned out to be quite satisfying. Coming and going on my own schedule, doing what I wanted when I wanted to and having the time to attend to my own needs was very relaxing and enjoyable. Between engrossing myself in my work and spending time off with my kids back in eastern Pennsylvania, I was happy and content with life. Thankfully, my mental health continued to remain totally in check as I ventured into a new life of bachelorhood. Meeting new friends in the Pittsburgh area helped me improve my social life and brought a sense of wholeness to my previous feelings of abandonment.

A young woman who was a supervisor of flight attendant training was actively searching for a place to live near our company's offices. Sarah Hutchinson owned a house in southern Virginia, and was interested in a finding a convenient place to stay while working during the week in the Pittsburgh area. Sarah actually helped me look at my eventual new home, and when I offered the spare bedroom in my recently purchased townhouse, she accepted the invitation without hesitation. It was great having such a fine young lady as my "roomy" and she provided some very close companionship during my budding bachelor independence. In my opinion, we made extremely compatible roommates. Her monthly contribution toward expenses helped me with my mortgage payment, and it was a pleasure to have a young woman's perspective around from time to time. We both worked busy schedules and our weekend travel demands did not allow us a whole lot of time together at my place. During the work week, occasionally we would both be at the house at the same time, and we would spend the evening taking out many of the frustrations we experienced from our infant airline division's growing pains. Just having Sarah there and being able to communicate with someone while still experiencing some left over hurt from my recently broken marriage was extremely therapeutic and a true blessing.

Our personal and professional relationships remained strong and although I would have liked our friendship to grow into something more, she was already spoken for. The relationship we shared was strictly plutonic, and today she is happily married to the man in her life back then. Sarah moved out of my townhouse after tendering her resignation with our mutual employer and accepting a flight attendant position at a new and upcoming airline. As she left for JetBlue Airways, I was tremendously indebted to her for the wonderful companionship she provided while being my roommate and for contributing to my continued saneness in the frustrating aftermath of my second failed marriage.

"Sarah, thank you for all the warm smiles, your always caring attitude and a very supportive friendship. I am

so glad we had the opportunity to get to know each other a little better. May you and Jonathan be richly blessed with much happiness and a healthy family when that time comes... Peace!"

Additionally, during this time of my newfound bachelor freedom, I was fortunate enough to travel to many interesting places with my two boys. The most notable trips included flying into Las Vegas, then driving to the Grand Canyon and making multiple trips to Washington State to visit close friends. Deborah Kerr had been the Manager of Training Records at the airline where I had instructed a few years back in Middletown, Pennsylvania. From working closely together, Deb and I developed a special friendship that has lasted to this day. She had recently married a gentleman from the same area and her new husband, Bradley, accepted a job transfer to the adventurous Northwest.

They originally moved to Roslyn, Washington while building their woodland dream house just off Route 97 in Cle Elum. Brydon and I flew into Seattle-Tacoma International Airport, where the happy couple picked us up and took us over the Snoqualmie Pass via Interstate 90 into their exciting new world. We spent several days relaxing in the tranquility surrounding their spacious, all-wood home that bordered National Forrest. We accomplished a float trip down the magnificent Yakima River and even visited Mount Rainier on our way back to the Seattle airport. I have visited Deb and Brad several times, and each time upon arriving at their majestic home, we are always made to feel like family. These two marvelous friends always seem anxious for our visits, and I am very grateful to them for sharing their little slice of heaven with us.

At work, some restructuring changes were necessary to meet the growing needs of our regional airline division. I was transferred to a new position, a lateral move of sorts, joining the flight training department from my former position as the Ground School Supervisor. As a Flight Training Analyst, I was introduced to one of the most influential and respected individuals I have ever had the pleasure of knowing. The gentleman now responsible for overseeing all that I did was Captain Ronald Sennam. Ron was a retired pilot from our parent company and was appointed the acting Director of Training and although he was my boss, he never made me feel like a subordinate and always treated me with the utmost respect. His ability to accomplish tasks with amazing charisma and his constant willingness to go above and beyond to exceed expectations was phenomenal.

Ron was a former Thunderbird[21] pilot, and it was apparent from the first time that I laid eyes on him that he was no ordinary guy. The twinkle in his eye and the aura of energy surrounding him were obvious clues that Ron was truly a special individual. His leadership qualities and outstanding ability to see through roadblocks were remarkable and it was a distinct honor to have served under his watch. I always joked with him that when he became President of the United States, he was to hold a cabinet level position open for me.

After a short while, my "Thunderbird" friend and mentor left the division to pursue other opportunities and his departing recommendations to the Vice President of Flight Operations were that I was highly capable and most qualified to assume the vacant role of Director. However, the decision was made to look outside the company for a replacement, and my new boss was hired several months later. I helped this newly hired director get comfortable with his new role and the surrounding politics that accompanied his new position. Training one's own boss is often a difficult task, but I helped get him up to speed

[21] A member of the United States Air Force precision flying team known as the Thunderbirds that performed aerobatics and formation flying exhibitions at air shows all over the world

because I liked this individual and I had been and remain a true team player. However, several weeks after he started, he was asked to tender his resignation over a job performance issue that probably could have been handled in a more caring and employee-supportive manner. With his departure, I was asked to take on additional responsibilities to make up for the void created by the new director's untimely departure.

I assumed the role of Supervisor of Training Records and Training Scheduling, stepping up to the new challenge with enthusiasm and professionalism. Managing the scheduling functions and overseeing record keeping while still accomplishing my responsibilities coordinating, developing and maintaining the flight training curriculum was a significant undertaking. When asked to take on these additional responsibilities, I agreed to do my best but felt somewhat betrayed by my superior who had previously decided to look outside the company when filling the open director position. The increased workload was graciously accepted, but I was discontented by the fact that I was accomplishing most of the same work once assigned to my short-tenured boss. I still had not received any promotional considerations or corresponding salary increases from the company. I began to lose any remaining motivation, and the previous inner drive that inspired me toward excellence had all but faded away. I had not considered that perhaps I was too young or viewed as too new on the block. At any rate, I no longer felt like I was a valued team member of our fledgling organization.

Our airline division began to experience some significant financial difficulties, and my job satisfaction continued to dwindle. Job responsibilities increased as the funds available to fairly compensate many of us in our expanding roles were non-existent. As I assumed greater duties and more responsibility, Frank Piper, our division's Chief Pilot, would joke with me that my new title should be "Slash." He used this term to sarcastically highlight the many slash marks and added job functions after my official position of Flight Training Analyst. Frank could not remember all that I was now responsible for, hence he simply called me "Slash" at times. I would occasionally end my e-mail messages to him simply signing with a " / " to illustrate the growing frustrations of my position. Frank and I had known each other for several years, and working together at the new division allowed us to become close friends. Frank and his family live in State College, Pennsylvania, and my Father has a mountain cabin just over the ridge from their home. I visit Frank on occasion when I get up that way and am very thankful for his continued friendship. He was a true confidant throughout my entire separation and impending divorce.

Our many dinners together through the work week, while we were both in the Pittsburgh area, focused on my relationship woes when we were not discussing the complexities and difficulties at work. Frank was very inspirational and his constant encouragement gave me continued hope when the anxiety from my marital frustrations seemed impossible to cope with. He is also an avid outdoorsman, and our mutual love for nature allowed me to escape the pain and reality of my broken marriage by talking about our daily wildlife sightings as well as past and present hunting adventures. On a few occasions, we were even able to spend some time together after work fishing a few local trout streams. Frank's friendship and support during some very difficult personal times provided a calming peace to my troubled soul, allowing my mental health to remain in check, even under measurable trying circumstances.

"Frank, you helped me weather storms on more than one occasion and encouraged me to laugh when I could have broken down and cried. For all your support and

companionship, I am eternally grateful. See you in Happy Valley soon my friend..."

As 2004 came to a close, it was obvious that our floundering airline division was headed in an undesirable direction. The job satisfaction I once felt had completely vanished, and my employment became simply a means of sustenance only. Although, I enjoyed living in western Pennsylvania and had developed some very good friendships, the inevitable was obvious and I realized the time had come for me to aggressively search for employment elsewhere. Shortly after finalizing the decision to look for another job, I was notified that my position in Pittsburgh would soon be transferred to the company's main training facility located in Charlotte, North Carolina. After learning of the impending relocation, I immediately put my townhouse on the real estate market and began to focus on finding a new career opportunity with another airline.

Around this time, Frederick Carnell, a former check airman and pilot who worked with me in Pittsburgh, sent me an important e-mail regarding a job opportunity. Frederick advised me that his new employer was actively searching to hire career flight training instructors, and he had recommended me to his supervisor as an excellent candidate. He supplied me with the Manager of Continuous Training's e-mail address and encouraged me to make immediate contact. After sending a message to the training manager and later speaking with him on the phone for some time, he expressed considerable interest in my qualifications. Acting on Frederick's recommendation, the training manager, Sam Stinson, carefully laid out a time schedule for me to follow if I were truly interested in pursuing an instructor position with this fairly new, rising airline company.

I was told to go on the company's website and fill out an official application, and after that was completed, an interview would be arranged. I completed the on-line application process and was called for an interview. Traveling to Miami, Florida, for the job interview, I met Sam and several other individuals including personnel people and the Director of Training for the new company. I felt the interview went well but was somewhat concerned with the Director of Training's apprehension over my lack of recent flight experience. I immediately called Captain Sennam, my previous supervisor and mentor to request a huge favor. Ron had recently had some contact with some of the individuals in the training department at this new company, and I asked him to make a call to the director to discuss my work performance and flying skills which he had personally witnessed several months prior while we were in Montreal, Canada.

After returning home from south Florida, I drafted thank you letters to the individuals I had met and sent a package via overnight delivery so it would arrive at the Miami Training Center first thing the following morning. The next day, shortly before 11:00 AM, I received a call from Sam Stinson saying he had just opened the overnight letter and read my correspondence. He told me they were impressed with my attitude and skills and was excited to say that they were preparing to make me a job offer. He was looking forward to bringing me on board and informed me that the airline's personnel department was preparing an official offer of employment pending results of my background investigation. Apparently any apprehensions that existed about my flying experience had been resolved, thanks to the phone call from my previous boss and good friend, Ron. After successful completion of the background check and passing a pre-employment drug and alcohol screening, the offer letter arrived. I felt very fortunate to be selected and gratefully accepted the position of Simulator Instructor with this premier air carrier.

My townhouse in Imperial, Pennsylvania, sold as I was involved in the interviewing process for the prospective company. I planned on moving all my belongings into storage until my future living arrangements were arranged and house closing was scheduled for December 30, 2004. Everything went as scheduled, and I was able to start 2005 off with money in the bank, and a bright new employment outlook. I excitedly tendered my resignation to my current employer and arranged for a one week sabbatical between jobs to spend some valuable time with my two boys. Resigning from this position that had created some high levels of stress and growing frustrations felt completely liberating. It seemed like as if the weight of the world had been lifted from my shoulders and I was ecstatic! On January 17, 2005, I began a southward migration to my new position in the warmth of Florida's winter sunshine.

Initial training for this new career opportunity would take place in Miami, Florida. Although the new company offered to pay for air transportation to Miami, I elected to take my personal vehicle to Florida with me by booking a reservation onboard the Amtrak AutoTrain™. I drove to Lorton, Virginia to meet the train for a late afternoon departure and was both excited and relaxed as the train pulled slowly out of the station shortly after 4:00 PM. A few hours into the trip, scheduled for eighteen hours, the constant thumping of the rails beneath us eased to silence as the train crawled to a stop. The conductor announced that ahead of the southbound locomotive, unscheduled railway repair had closed the tracks and that we would be delayed approximately one hour. We had stopped near Glen Allen, Virginia, remarkably very close to where I had lived in my first home some fourteen years before.

After nearly an hour had passed and once receiving the all clear signal, the train lurched forward as it began to move, slowly increasing its speed. The shrill of the blowing whistle was audible as we approached the intersection close to my old neighborhood. The sharp sound of the train's whistle instantly brought back memories of when I used to hear the late night whistles from my bedroom of the passing trains which had become soothing as I drifted in and out of my once restful nights. Later on, the whistles of the passing trains served as a reminder of how little time had gone by in my often sleepless nights during the onset of my initial depressive episode. As we continued to accelerate, I could barely make out the houses lining the little cult-de-sac on in the dim street lit evening. I did capture a brief glimpse of the small white rancher where my first wife and I had lived in the Richmond area. The home in which we welcomed our son Brydon into the world and where I persevered the devastating effects of the darkness that had engulfed my life many years earlier. My mind was flooded with vivid memories from my life back then, when I experienced both joy and heartache in this first home of mine. I thought it quite ironic that the train tracks that once beckoned me to end my struggle with the dismal darkness were now carrying me to a promising new employment opportunity and a rejuvenated life in sunny Florida. As the train rolled on, I was able to relax and eventually rested quite comfortably as the repetitious thumping noise of the train passing the uneven tracks lulled me to sleep.

The train pulled into Sanford, Florida, on the morning of January 18th, and I anxiously waited for my vehicle to be unloaded from the large, auto-carrying train cars. It took a few hours until my Chevy Cavalier made its way to the claiming area, and I hopped in and headed eastbound toward Interstate 95 South. After nearly five hours of driving, I arrived at the hotel in Miami where I was to stay and attend a poolside social event prior to starting my first day of employment with the new company. Getting to meet my fellow training classmates and many of the leadership individuals from this magnificent company that evening was a truly exciting and uplifting experience. The next morning, January 19, 2005, I officially began my tenure as a Pilot Instructor for this industry-leading airline corporation. I was elated to become a crewmember with this truly dynamic, outstanding and people-focused organization. I felt quite fortunate to have been selected to fill an open instructing position with this highly respected and very successful aviation enterprise.

My initial training was exactly the same as that of the company's newly hired pilots. My classmates and I attended a thorough four-week program in which we were all checked out as First Officers. Being hired to serve as a simulator instructor, I then entered a condensed training course in preparation for my Airbus 320 Captain's check ride. On April 2, 2005, I received my A320 Type Rating. My advanced training continued to become qualified to eventually teach on this transport category aircraft. After completing training and working as an instructor for several months in Miami, the corporation's training activities would be moving north to a newly constructed facility in Orlando.

In March of 2005, I scheduled a trip to the Orlando area to look for a home that would be ready or available by June, our tentative relocation date. After looking at several places, I was able to locate a new condominium community in Vista Lakes that was just five miles from the new training facility, still under construction. I was shown a first floor, two bedroom unit under construction and immediately decided that this would suit my needs perfectly. Having had money in the bank from the sale of my Imperial townhouse last December, I placed a deposit on the property and planned to take possession of my new home sometime in July or August. I worked in Miami until the 3rd of June and packed my belongings into my little blue Cavalier and set out on my northward journey to the "Land of the Famous Mouse."

My new company arranged for me to stay in a nearby hotel for the month of June because of my condo still being under construction. As we moved into our training center at the Orlando International Airport, the facility was immaculate and drew a lot of attention as many prominent community leaders and even Florida's Governor Jeb Bush attended the official opening ceremony. Training in the spacious, newly-constructed building was and remains a wonderful experience and instills great pride from being able to work in such a splendid, state-of-the-art facility. Furthermore, the people in this organization are truly outstanding in their field and a real pleasure to work with. Having the opportunity to work with so many talented and spirited individuals has been quite invigorating and heart-warming for me.

After my month was up in the company-supplied hotel, I moved to Celebration, Florida, with one of the other instructors I worked with. He had rented a beautiful lakefront home near downtown Celebration[22] and invited me to stay with him until my condominium was completed. Robert Wolram was and is a very generous man and we have developed a fairly close friendship. He is a few years my senior, and I often looked up to him with great respect and humility. The time I spent in his home was very relaxing and enjoyable. One of the best benefits was the ability to walk out the front door of the house and be in downtown Celebration in only minutes. Also, the many miles of scenic walking paths of beautiful pines and oaks allowed me to enjoy the beauty of the outdoors while getting much needed exercise during daily walks around the surrounding lakes. I eventually was able to get my first glimpses of the elusive Florida alligator on some of my walks around the community paths.

---

[22] Celebration, FL, is a small, quaint community that was originally designed by Walt Disney to emulate his ideal "town concept" patterned after his boyhood experiences.

Robert and I were able to dine out often and enjoyed many good times together, even cooking dinner one evening for two women who he had met at a nearby mall. The dinner went well, we all had fun chatting and more importantly, I was able to meet a wonderful woman named Jan Foyer. Jan had actually dated Robert for a short time, but she and I would become the best of friends over time. Jan, who was considerably older than me and had recently divorced, experienced some difficult times after being unjustly terminated from her position as an elementary school teacher for over thirty years.

I have come to believe our paths were destined to cross so that I could be supportive of her during some trying times, and she would likewise supply my life with additional "light". Her motherly instincts and tremendous energy levels fostered our friendship to grow into something truly special. After inviting me to Sunday services at her church, we became truly giving spiritual friends. Over time, our friendship has developed into a very unique and caring relationship. Once we sat in a hot car and talked for hours about the lowest of times when the Holy Spirit was the most present in our lives. I also recently joined the Orlando area United Methodist Church she introduced me to.

Many times in previous years, I had requested accommodation from the Federal Aviation Administration (FAA) and was repeatedly denied a "Special Issuance" medical certificate to return to my career. In the early summer of 2005, with my bipolar condition still totally in check, a close associate and aviation flight surgeon who had been helping me pursue my case for many years gave me a call. Dr. Donald Houston was quite familiar with my situation and has led efforts to formally petition the FAA into allowing individuals like myself to have flight privileges re-instated following such long periods of mental stability. His phone call began with some small talk because it had been some time since we had last talked and continued with Doc Houston informing me of some interesting news. It appeared I would be getting my medical certificate back soon because a change in the FAA's position regarding my condition was pending.

I was very excited and yet cautiously optimistic about this new door that had seemingly opened. He explained that the Federal Air Surgeon's office had decided to let a handful of individuals into a "pilot program" that would allow us to fly while monitoring our performance and progress for about one year. If all went well and my health remained unchanged during this oversight period, I would be eligible for an unrestricted medical certificate that essentially would put my piloting career back on track. All that was needed was a few meetings to discuss the specifics and establish the protocol for the new program, and most likely by Thanksgiving I would be eligible to return to the flight deck if I chose to resume that career path again. I was elated to hear this great news and could hardly wait to hear from him later in the year.

I also anxiously waited the day when I would be able to move into my condominium home which was nearing the end of its construction. Work as a flight instructor was going well and with the ability to fly free of charge, I was able to be with Brydon and Alex a fair amount of time. On my scheduled days off, I would scurry to the airport to catch a plane out of Orlando heading northbound to Philadelphia, Pennsylvania, or Baltimore, Maryland. Once I arrived at one of the northern destinations, I would either pick up a rental car or hop a train ride into Lancaster to spend time with my children and parents. Occasionally, I would arrange to have my folks pick me up at one of the airports or at the train station from time to time. After arriving in Lancaster, by plane, train or automobile, I would keep my two sons with me for a few days, usually staying at my parents' house. Every now and then, the three of us would spend some time down at my brother's place or take a trip to the mountains for a weekend.

As my oldest boy was now a teenager, he was increasingly involved in extra curricular activities, and many of my visits consisted of Alex and me attending Brydon's sporting events. Even though I lived over a thousand miles away from my children, it was apparent I was now able to spend more time with my kids than when I was working in Pittsburgh where previously I had only weekends off. During the most recent year, I was able to attend several football and basketball games without taking any extra time off from work. I thoroughly enjoyed my job and with the added benefit of being able to see my boys more often, life was exceptionally good!

My condominium closing was scheduled for August 26, 2005, so I began to make arrangements to have my personal belongings moved to my soon to be new home in Orlando, Florida. After getting several quotes and even looking at renting a self-move large hauling truck, I was able to locate a freight company that would drop off a trailer at my packing location and transport my entire earthly belongings down the east coast for a very reasonable price. I scheduled the U Pack™ truck trailer to be parked at the storage facility where my personal property had been stored for the past eight months. I headed north to Lancaster to oversee the packing process and the initial movement of my belongings. With the help of my Father, brothers and limited help from our kids, we finished the task of loading my furniture, clothing, golf clubs, bicycle and various household items in only a few hours.

As we loaded the last few pieces of my property, Brydon prepared my mountain bike for loading by inflating the tires to normal pressure and anxiously waited for the okay signal to ride the bicycle up the ramp onto the trailer. As he raced toward the loading ramp, I could not help but remember the years when riding my bike up similar inclines gave me such tremendous thrills. He successfully ascended the ramp and was able to stop the bike before colliding into the forward section of the trailer where all my possessions were securely packed. After installing the plywood barriers and load binders, I called the freight company to come and pick up the trailer which would be filled with other shipments scheduled to arrive the Orlando area in three to four days. My Dad, brothers and our kids went out for a family dinner at a local restaurant, where I picked up the tab as an appreciative token for their help in my big move. After dinner, we returned to the storage facility and let the truck driver through the gate to hook up to the trailer and pull it from the storage lot on its initial journey that would hopefully end at my new condo in central Florida. As the tractor trailer hauling all my belongings pulled away from the storage units and headed down the road, I wished my possessions a safe and healthy trip.

Once I arrived back in Orlando, final inspection of my condominium was completed and closing went on as scheduled. In the afternoon of August 26th, I moved into a new, bare two bedroom condo that was now my Orlando home. Actually, the mortgage company owned it, and I was only the person responsible for making the monthly payments. A few days later, the trailer I had packed back in Pennsylvania pulled into the condominiums was unhooked and left for me to unload. It was a relief to see that my belongings safely arrived and with the help of a few good friends from work, mainly a fellow instructor named Carlisle, the trailer was unloaded. With my personal property moved into the previously empty dwelling, my once barren condo began to take on the appearance of a home. After several days of unpacking boxes and arranging my belongings, my new home felt warm, inviting and complete.

The newly finished condominium suited my needs perfectly, was convenient to my workplace and turned out to be a very smart and timely investment. Shortly after settling into my new place, I agreed to take on a roommate. Mark Herr had worked with me as a Check

Airman at our previous employer and was also a fellow instructor at our new company. His easy going manner and hard work ethics allowed the two of us to get along rather well and he made quite a compatible roommate. His home was in Charlotte, North Carolina, and when he was working in Orlando, he would stay with me at the condo and even have his fiancée visit from time to time. Mark's company at the house has allowed us to become good friends.

In October, our company initiated service to the Newark Liberty International Airport from Orlando. This new service to Newark, New Jersey, was now the closest airport to my hometown of Lancaster, Pennsylvania, to which our growing airline had flights arriving. I decided to purchase a second vehicle to make my commuting between Florida and Pennsylvania easier. After I decided on an Audi Quattro for my Florida transportation needs, my Dad flew down to Orlando for a few days and accompanied me northward in my Cavalier that I now intended to keep at the airport in Newark. Having the flexibility to catch up to five flights a day on my own airline and having dependable and reliable transportation on both ends of my commute allowed for a more relaxed and enjoyable travel experience.

With my multi-car transportation system in place, I no longer relied upon my parents to pick me up or drop me off regularly at area airports. However, they were still willing to provide airport transportation to me once in a while, if I requested shuttle service. My mom and dad, known as "Pappy" and "Grandma" to my kids, are fantastic as they still regularly pick up my youngest boy Alex and have him comfortably settled in their home when I arrive from my six-hour commute from central Florida. Thanks to my loving parents, I am able to spend more quality time with my boys due to their willingness to shuttle Alex and Brydon to and from their mothers.

Having heard nothing from Dr. Houston regarding the reinstatement of my pilot medical certificate, I decided to give him a call to check on the status of the program he informed me of earlier in the year. I immediately knew something was wrong by the tone of his voice. He told me that the Federal Air Surgeon's office had done a complete about face of their former stance and decided not to undertake any changes after all. The official answer was that the program was postponed pending the outcome of a new study being conducted by the National Institute of Health dealing with psychotropic medication and its affects on adolescents. How this new study correlates to or affects my case after nearly twelve years of complete stability, was quite uncertain. After all these years of waiting and listening to the FAA's bureaucratic excuses, what harm in waiting a while longer?

Dr. Houston is one of the brightest minds in the aviation medical arena and he has assured me that I will fly again. With his inside view of the situation, he advises me that when the current leadership at the FAA Medical Office steps down, monumental change will most likely be right around the corner. I can only hope and pray that the Federal Air Surgeon, who has played God with my case for the last twelve years, will decide that after thirty plus years of government service, it is time for him to retire. Reshaping the archaic views of this medical review branch might allow the winds of change to blow through the agency; hopefully, opening eyes and minds to remarkable advances that have taken place in the dynamically changing field of medicine.

Twice in the month of November, I scheduled trips to visit some great friends in the Pittsburgh, Pennsylvania, area and to do some traditional Pennsylvania whitetail buck hunting. The first trip was for archery hunting early in the month, and the second trip just after Thanksgiving, was for rifle hunting and extended into the first few days of December. I had met Ed and Kathy Winters while working in

Pittsburgh with my previous employer several years earlier. Ed worked for a private contractor that maintained the computers at the airline, and his wife Kathy worked as a Passenger Service Representative at the Greater Pittsburgh International Airport. Shortly after meeting Ed in the fall of 2002, while working on my office computer, we started talking about hunting and quickly realized the we had reached some common ground. He told me about his place in Beaver County and the acreage that accompanied it. I was excited to here about his little piece of western Pennsylvania paradise, and he invited me out to go hunting sometime. I did not hesitate to take him up on the invitation and as we started hunting together our friendship grew.

Today, Ed, Kathy, their son Shane, and their big black lab Stanley are some of the most important friends with whom I have ever been blessed. I now refer to their home as the "Winters' Bed & Breakfast" because of the wonderful hospitality they continually show me. Ed's companionship and our adventures together in the woods surrounding his home coupled with Kathy's tremendous cooking during my stays causes me to think of Beaver County, Pennsylvania, as a slice of heaven. The peace, solitude and pure enjoyment that I experience when I travel to my favorite "B & B" are astounding. I don't know where else on earth I could find such gracious hospitality and also have a 110 lb., licking black alarm clock. Stan is a great dog and he is always excited to see his good buddy from central Florida. I was unsuccessful during this year's hunting trips but thoroughly enjoyed the time spent with my trustworthy friends. I thank God continually to have met such fine people and I anxiously await my next hunting trip and visit to my dear friends.

As the Christmas holiday season approached, I planned to have Alex and Brydon come to Florida for the week between Christmas and New Year's Day to stay with me in my condo for the first time. I invited my parents to come along to supervise the children while I was scheduled to work a few days during this time period. We had a fine time, even though "Pappy" had a very bad cold most of the week. We spent two days touring the Kennedy Space Center, and I was even able to take my entire family into the simulator at work for a mock flight around the New York City area. I gave my mom and my oldest son Brydon some instructional lessons on flying the Airbus 320. Brydon did a very nice job, probably attributed to his experience with video games,[23] and even accomplished a wonderful landing all by himself as I reminded him occasionally to make the proper stick inputs. "Grandma," however, was a different story.

As I attempted to talk her through her first takeoff and told her to pull back on the side stick, I neglected to include the key word "gently" in my instructions. As she firmly grasped the stick and hauled it fully aft, the aircraft rotated rapidly skyward and we all heard the loud banging noise as the simulator replicated the sound of the aircraft tail striking the runway as we became airborne. Needless to say, I only allowed my mother to witness the aircraft's remarkable automatic landing capabilities as we gently settled onto the runway at JFK International Airport.

Only through the ability of modern computerization, I made the required inputs to reposition the simulator to the Seattle-Tacoma International Airport where we took off and flew toward Mount Rainier, towering over 14,000 feet. After flying around the northwest for several minutes we ended the simulator session. Little Alex was overwhelmed that we were still in Orlando when we exited the big white "box" after having flown in several parts of the country for nearly an hour. I am

---

[23] The Airbus 319/320/321 family of aircraft is flown by a Side Stick Controller requiring the gentle skill similar to manipulating a joy stick found in many popular video games today.

sure that the realism of the simulator and the ability to reposition aircraft geographical location by a single push of the button was quite difficult for a four-year-old's mind to comprehend. After repeated explanations, I think he was able to understand the big picture. God loves the innocence of a child! We should all nurture and relish the simplistic views of our little ones.

As the New Year 2006 was ushered in, my life was quite happy and I was very content for the most part. Alex turned five on January 8th and shortly after I reached my forty-first birthday. Officially, I was "over the hill" and now seemed to be headed down the other side. Brydon turned fourteen at the end of February, and my entire family was doing remarkably well as we were all blessed with wonderful health and much happiness. Between working in Orlando, traveling to New York to teach an occasional recurrent pilot ground school and spending time in Pennsylvania with my children and family, life was extremely fast-paced yet rewarding. I was and remain forever grateful for the many blessings bestowed on my loved ones and myself. I continue to live life to the fullest and proceed one day at a time.

Currently, I am able to enjoy a perfectly normal life and at the present time experience no negative effects whatsoever from the inherited illness that once took me to the brink of self-destruction. I can only hope and pray that the engulfing darkness never returns, but I am quite confident that the worst battles in my life have already been fought. I know that life has no guarantees and that my remaining years will most likely not be a smooth voyage. The rough seas I have already endured only served to make me a stronger and wiser person. From this developed strength and wisdom, I am certain that with God as my Captain, I can weather any future storms that might be placed in my path. Also, I am hopeful that in time, I will be able to return to the cockpit resuming my pilot career once changes are initiated within the Federal Aviation Administration. By the grace of God, I have been able to rise triumphantly above the dark storm clouds that once completely drowned out the sunshine in my life. The smothering darkness eventually gave way to an amazing spiritual journey filled with light, hope and true happiness. These factual accounts of a personal evolution have illustrated an astounding revival that I have termed my *Ascent from Darkness.*

CHAPTER THIRTEEN
REFLECTIONS

As I look back on all that has happened in my life to this point, today's reality is that I am fortunate enough to live with an inherited mental illness that has little if any detrimental effect on my daily activities. The bipolar disorder that I was diagnosed with in 1993 is completely controlled by the medication I have taken for many years and the faith I have grown to know in an amazingly gracious God. I experience no unpleasant or uncomfortable side effects from the lithium carbonate controlled-release tablets that I continue to take twice a day. I have personally witnessed and have read many stories about individuals who feel they no longer need the medication so vitally important to controlling mood disorders. Many individuals somehow decide to discontinue taking this valuable stabilizing agent, and often the discontinuation of the needed medication leads to tragic circumstances.

I feel wholeheartedly, the continued success in managing my inherited illness rests upon the realization that in order to lead a full, healthy and normal life, I must continue on the medication probably for the rest of my life. I will never be cured of my condition, but I have learned to accept its place in my life and have risen above it.

With the help of loving family and friends, caring counselors, fantastic physicians, some true guardian angels and my ever-growing trust in a truly magnificent God, I am adequately armed to face anything life brings my way. I have weathered a ferocious storm and pray that the worst is behind me, but I rest assured that God will give me the strength to meet additional challenges that might surface in my uncharted future.

I have learned a tremendous amount about the disorder that I'll carry with me the rest of my life. Bipolar disorder can be a very devastating illness for many, but fortunately my condition was receptive to treatment. I am now able to live a symptom free, productive life. Many individuals combating serious mental illnesses are not as fortunate in their personal struggles with the darkness inducing abnormalities of the mind, and I sympathize with their sometimes overwhelming plights. If you are one of these individuals, maintain a disciplined mental toughness and repeatedly tell yourself that your condition will not keep you in the challenging darkness forever.

From my life experiences and a personal walk through the lowest depths of the darkness, I have theorized a strategy for sustaining hope and eventually winning over paralyzing depression. I believe the keys to success in protecting one's mental well-being while suffering through a serious illness of the mind rests in a principle I call the "Mental Wellness Triangle." Perseverance during severe bouts of depression can prove to be one of the biggest struggles of an individual's life if the darkness strikes. Hanging in there while waiting for relief and eventually triumphing over a devastating affliction can be realized by employing the concepts of this important triad or MWT Model (see diagram).

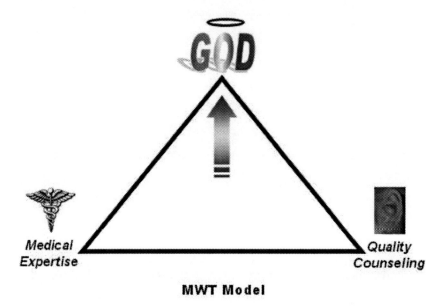

MWT Model

The importance of receiving quality medical treatment by a board certified physician is paramount. Keep in mind the fact that some of our nation's doctors graduated in the lower echelons of their medical school classes, yet still received a diploma and a license to practice medicine.[24] A physician who lacks attention to detail and a driving pursuit of excellence can be a huge anchor weighing down one's recovery during critical times. Thoroughly research a physician if you feel any reservations about the quality of care you receive, and find someone new if you are not happy with the pace of progress. An aggressive psychiatrist honed to take advantage of the latest in modern psychological techniques and medications will increase the overall chances of quicker stabilization and ultimately a successful recovery for patients.

---

[24] This statement is not meant to question the validity of state licensing or medical school standards but merely illustrates the point that even mediocre individuals can and do practice medicine.

All too often, financial concerns and a lack of adequate medical insurance coverage can create additional hardships. Psychiatric care and psychological counseling is terribly expensive and fees continue to escalate. Many physicians and mental health facilities will work with you if financial barriers exist, and sliding scale rate structures have been put in place at some institutions. However, one will usually have to search out these caring professionals and helpful organizations from the rest of the lot. Checking with your local Mental Health Services office or a local chapter of the National Alliance for the Mentally Ill (NAMI) will give you some guidance on locating affordable mental healthcare.

Write your elected leaders, mainly your local United States Congressperson and the Senators representing your state asking them to pass legislation guaranteeing mental health parity. Prospective laws have been introduced and debated for many years, but the time has come for our leaders to enact important statutes mandating equality among mental health and physical health issues. Parity will also help defer some of the stigma and discriminatory practices surrounding illnesses of the mind. Recently, I applied for discounted life insurance through a group term policy offer. Although I had been symptom free for over twelve years and continue to experience no detrimental effects from my bipolar illness whatsoever, disclosing my condition generated a denial letter. This major insurer did explain how I might qualify for insurance upon re-application; however, the premiums would be significantly higher then those advertised in the offer letter due to my bipolar diagnosis.

Making competent medical care available and affordable to all Americans hampered with debilitating mental illnesses are necessities to our social structure. Every individual needs to be assured of the basic right to adequate medical attention when an illness of the mind is the diagnosis. A foundation of the MWT Model mandates the importance of proper medical treatment and its crucial role in returning individuals to wholeness and making them productive members of our society once again. Untreated mental health issues, mainly depression, cause far too many people to prematurely end their lives. The cost to the American economy for untreated mental illness is astonishing. We must do a better job in helping the citizens of this nation who are pressured by high healthcare costs and increasing levels of stress brought on by a less than caring system.

The second critical leg of the wellness triangle is access to quality counseling. During deep valleys in one's life, a highly skilled psychological counselor can bring needed comfort and offer effective strategies to persevere and eventually overcome the often engulfing darkness. Psychotherapy has proven effective for many individuals suffering from all kinds of emotional pain and life struggles. Its importance in helping individuals with bona fide illnesses of the mind cannot be understated. Quality professional counselors that offer productive soul-searching and valuable coping mechanisms are worth their weight in gold. Pastors, ministers and priests often provide limited counseling services and one's economical situation may mandate exclusive use of these services. Please realize that if your situation is serious, a well-trained professional counselor or psychologist is essential in training one's mind to combat the "slings and arrows" of self-defeat often associated with a darkness inducing illness.

The final triad and the precipice in the MWT Model is a firm belief in a higher power that can accomplish *anything*. God works in mysterious ways, and His total love is real and unconditional for all of His children. Remember: No matter what color skin you have, what part of the earth you are from nor what religion you practice, acknowledging the infinite power of one almighty, all knowing God will give you the strength to carry on and help alleviate your suffering if

183

you take all your concerns to Him in fervent prayer. Building your faith through reading the scriptures and various faith based motivational books will act as powerful weapons in fighting the dreaded darkness which drains away happiness.

If you commit your entire self to God's care, you will be amazed at the strength He provides in your time of need and in the darkest of hours. In my opinion, from my education and life experiences, trust in God is the most important part of the Mental Wellness Triangle. His presence is depicted at the top of the MWT Model to emphasize this importance and to serve as a reminder that He provides the framework and the glue that holds the Triangle together. Keep in mind that the mental wellness model has three important points, all three serving an irreplaceable function, but the pinnacle of the triangle is your own belief, trust and faith in a God who cares about you and will help return your body and soul to wholeness.

If you are currently engulfed in the darkness, work tirelessly to get plugged into the lifesaving foundations of the Mental Wellness Triangle. Make sure you are receiving aggressive, competent medical care and productive, caring counseling. Should you have any doubt as to the quality of care you are receiving, explore changes in your medical treatment and psychological counseling. Work continuously to cultivate your spiritual relationship with our heavenly Father. God knows the extent of your suffering and hears your desperate pleas for help, and He will deliver you from the depths of darkness if you place total trust in Him and be patient. Please be aware that there are both good and evil forces in our universe. When God cast one of His most powerful angels out of heaven, the eternal struggle began. Remember that the leader of the fallen spirits, Satan himself, loves to prey upon a weary soul and will attempt to pull you into the downward spiral of unending despair. Fight "the evil one" with all your heart, mind and soul, and God will provide the strength to see you through your lowest of times.

If you know someone caught in the unrelenting darkness, offer your assistance to help them get plugged into the Mental Wellness Triangle. Often individuals hampered with severe depression are so beaten down by such oppressive illnesses that their abilities to cope with life are sometimes totally obliterated. As a concerned friend or family member, take the steps previously described to make sure they are receiving the best of care or at least adequate care. Love for someone means not turning your back on them in this most desperate of times. I have seen friends and family turn away from loved ones afflicted with a mental illness simply because they could not or did not want to deal with the harsh realities. Get out of your comfort zone, educate yourself about illnesses of the mind that your loved one has affecting his or her life right now and get in the fight with them. You can become a true guardian angel to them and may even end up saving a life in the process. Pray for them continually and encourage others to say prayers as well. The power of prayer is phenomenal! God is very busy and in my opinion, the more calls he receives regarding one of His children in need, the more attention that individual will receive in overcoming the paralyzing effects of painful and debilitating illnesses of the mind.

From the time I began having serious trouble sleeping up to my fully recovered mental state and spiritually whole self today, I had no idea what turns my life would take as I journeyed down an unknown path. As the depression deepened early in my bout with the engulfing darkness, I felt hopeless and helpless to pull myself out of the depths of this hell on earth. Once I could no longer guarantee my own safety, the trip to the psychiatric hospital was desperately needed, yet serves as a powerful reminder of just how low one can get. That morning of my admittance to the psychiatric ward was one of the lowest points in my life. What scared me the most was the thought of not having my intelligent and gifted brain return again to a healthy, productive state, one that God had given me for most of my young life.

During the hospitalization my memory, cognitive reasoning functions and ability to concentrate were so severely impaired that I was a complete basket case. The tremendous love I had for my flying career that was not only a respectable source of income but an enjoyable hobby to boot brought me unbelievable heartache when it was obvious I would probably never fly again. Every fiber of my being was crushed as I saw no possible way of climbing out of an unfathomably deep pit. Walking on faith alone, I left that institution on a huge wing and a prayer.

Uttering the words I learned from an old Christmas classic,[25] "You put one foot in front of the other..." Step by step and day by day, I slowly pulled myself back to the top of that once insurmountable, dark hole. With the help of some wonderful physicians and the right medication, I was able to step out into the sunshine again that had been hidden from my soul for so long. I praise God every day for carrying me on that big wing and a prayer some fourteen years ago.

I encourage the many individuals who are presently caught up in their own struggles with the consuming darkness to stay in the game. Persevere until the day when the clouds part and the bright rays of hope and happiness return to your life. That day *will* come if you pray fervently, follow the advice of your physician and desperately hang onto your faith. God gives each of us the inner strength to make it through the toughest of times. Continually ask Him to keep that leader of the fallen spirits away from you and pray for the strength to withstand the "slings and arrows" that will be aimed at you. You must persevere,

---

[25] The timeless holiday program, "Santa Claus is Coming to Town" when Chris Kringle is teaching the Winter Warlock how to gracefully walk through the archway door

because triumphing over deep depression and the many illnesses of the mind that have haunted countless individuals over the course of history is possible. Leading a meaningful and fulfilling life is the dream of all humankind; however, the ultimate victory lies not in this world. By placing on a suit of armor that consists not only of friendships, good healthcare and medications, but primarily on the amazing power of God and "the Holy Spirit," living a relaxing and comfortable life in this world is within one's grasp.

I would like to relate a few personal sentiments in order to share my appreciation to the most significant individuals in my life and to allow this autobiographical account to be complete. From the bottom of my heart, I need to tell my first wife Andrea that I am eternally grateful for her seeing me through the early stages of this often crippling illness. I harbor no ill will toward her and commend her for fighting a valiant battle. The constant emotional drain from my deep depression and the often wild manic highs were just too big a roller coaster for both of us to stay on. I wish Andrea all the happiness this world has to offer and I thank her for being such a wonderful mother to our son Brydon.

> ""Andrea, you persevered through some gut wrenching times, and I harbor no ill will toward you. Thank you for seeing me through the darkest days of my trying ordeal and for being a great mother to our son. You were a true guardian angel and I will always cherish the memories of our happiness together before the engulfing darkness invaded my life. You will always occupy a very special place in my heart. My eternal love..."

The failure of my second marriage still weighs heavily on my soul, but I feel no bitterness toward Brenda either. I have turned all my frustrations and the surrounding confusion over to the Lord and I will pray continually for her. Her probable victimization stole the innocence from a dear little child at such an early age, and I ask God many times a day to help Brenda find her way in this world filled with hurt, but none more than her own. She continues to be a magnificent mother to our son Alex and I wish her total happiness in all her future endeavors. After my first divorce, she helped me learn how to once again live and experience life to the fullest. Our first few years were nearly dreamlike and the fond memories of our initial marriage will last a lifetime.

> *"Brenda, I truly appreciate all the wonderful times we shared before life's complexities stole the love from our relationship. Your dedication to being a great parent to our son Alex is commendable. Based on my beliefs, I hope in time you can reach some peace with whatever forces reside within you from your early childhood victimizations. My love always..."*

I want to once again honor my parents for being true warriors in not only my trials and tribulations, but for the total commitment to all four sons through the sorrows, heartaches and triumphs in our lives. After my big brother committed suicide, my parents grew stronger in their faith and provided immeasurable support to me during my period of severe mental illness. Most importantly was my mother. She provided the highest level of concern, understanding and love that any human being could possible give during my journey into the uncertainty of an illness of the mind. Her continuous support saw me through the worst of times when I was truly walking in "the Valley of the Shadow of Death." Mom's ability to listen and see me through the highs and lows of my bipolar experience was a true lifesaver. I cannot imagine going through this ordeal without such wonderfully devoted parents. God blessed me immensely by providing two of His best to bring me into this world, care for and nurture me and stand beside me when all hope was lost.

> *"Words cannot explain what I feel for the two of you. The light you provided <u>and</u> continue to provide in the life of your children and grandchildren is truly radiant. Your tremendous support and unconditional caring helped me survive the mammoth struggles associated with a very devastating mental illness. Your guiding presence allowed my eventual triumph over a hereditary condition that once drained the life from my body and caused me complete mental anguish. I cannot imagine my recovery and ensuing journey without you. You have certainly stored your treasures in the highest of places and may God continue to bless you richly till the day you enter the magnificent rooms set aside for you in the church triumphant. Well done Mom and Dad! All my love..."*

May my sons, Brydon and Alex, continue to be blessed with good health and much happiness. I live for these two young men, one a super student and athlete and the other an artistic and energetic towhead. I hope my life serves as a remarkable example of how a father should love his children. The example my parents have set for me will be carried on as a living legacy to their unyielding and relentless pursuit of being perfect, Godly parents. Being there for my boys as they face the inevitable uncertainties and unfairness of this world is and will remain a top priority of my life. Realizing the importance of helping others who are less fortunate is a valuable attribute I will attempt to instill into my sons' growing psyches. They both have had a good start in life, knowing the love of God and having two parents who love them dearly, even though their parents are no longer together. From early on in my two broken marriages, I each time had asked God to take the boys under His wing, and as the scripture verse states, "So have no fear, I myself will provide for you and your little ones" (Genesis 50:21), He has done so valiantly.

> *"Brydon and Alex, I love you two with all my heart and soul. You guys are my daily inspiration and I truly cherish you. Continue to learn, grow in your faith and carefully listen to the mystical voice of our heavenly Father in order to walk the path chosen for you. Attempt to maintain a sharp focus on your goals and may God bless you richly! I will continue to be the best father I can possibly be and realize that I will always be here for you. Please grow in your personal faith and let my experiences strengthen you in your times of sorrow. Focus all your efforts in life to the continual pursuit of goodness and truth and may your lights always help illuminate the darkness in this world. I am very proud of both of you! All my love..."*

May my life experiences and testimony, as chronicled in this memoir serve as a daily reminder that you, too, can win over depression and other often paralyzing disorders of the mind. I close my story with the words of one of God's most trustworthy servants, the Apostle Paul[26] as he had written in many of his scriptural letters, "May the God of love and peace be with you always!"

---

[26] Many biblical scholars have surmised that the "thorn in the side" Paul often wrote about or referred to in his writings were most likely attributed to possible recurring bouts of depression.

Printed in the United States
85987LV00008B/140/A